The Book On
Karuna
Reiki®

Advanced Healing Energy
for Our Evolving World

By Laurelle Shanti Gaia

Foreword by William Lee Rand

The Book On

Karuna Reiki®

Advanced Healing Energy
for Our Evolving World

ISBN 0-9678721-2-X

Published by:

Infinite Light Healing Studies Center, Inc

P.O. Box 130, Hartsel, CO 80449

www.infinitelight.com

Cover Design and Art by: Kwan Yin channeled by Laurelle Gaia

First printing June 2001
Second printing June 2002

A SPECIAL THANKS TO:

Copy editors

Virginia Krabbenhoft

Michael Arthur Baird

E. Barrie Kavasch

Book Design Consultant: Raymond D. Crites

Illustrator: Joan Rudholm

Note to the Reader

The techniques given in this book are intended as information, and not as a prescription. The stories shared here are anecdotal in nature and they have not been scientifically established. Therefore, neither the author nor the publisher can take responsibility for any positive or negative results, which may be produced by using these techniques.

The information and techniques described in this book are for the Karuna Reiki˙ student, or prospective student. This book is not meant to be an independent guide for self-healing. If you have a medical or psychological condition, the information in this book does not replace traditional medical or psychological treatment.

<u>The information in this book does not give the reader the ability to channel Karuna Reiki energy.</u> It is important to receive thorough training in a classroom situation under the supervision of a Registered Karuna Reiki˙ master teacher.

Dedication

This book is lovingly dedicated to:

Divine Love the only true power

To the masculine and feminine aspects of Divinity
in its many forms.

The enlightened beings who are guiding
humanity's awakening to the age of peace

The Lightweavers who choose to share this earth walk;
touching lives, opening hearts,
and aligning minds with the Divine.

Acknowledgements

I offer deep gratitude to my many spiritual teachers, those who assist me from the spiritual realms, and those who are incarnate now.

I am especially thankful to William Lee Rand, founder of the International Center for Reiki Training, and creator of Karuna Reiki. William continues to make a tremendous contribution to the Reiki community and to the world. He has been an inspiration to me for many years, and has always encouraged me to listen to my heart and follow the light of the Reiki energy.

I also thank the many students, clients and ICRT teachers who have studied and shared energy with me, and from whom I have learned so much. Through our sharing, we have all had opportunities to move forward on an accelerated path to peace.

I thank Nita Mocanu of Editions NIANDO for his dedication to the Reiki energy, which is evident through his teachings, publications, and simply being the light of Divine Love that he is. I appreciate his encouragement and support in the writing of this book.

My family has been supportive of my unusual ways, and I am forever thankful for their love.

A special thank you to my wonderful husband, Michael Arthur Baird, for his love, support, encouragement and help in bringing this book into manifestation.

About the Cover

When I was considering the design for the cover of this book many ideas surfaced. It was through the use of Karuna Reiki in prayer and meditation that the artwork for the cover of this book was inspired by Kwan Yin and ultimately created.

The lotus blossoms represent petals of wisdom as they gently open to reveal the purpose of our life and of all creation.

Two lotus blossoms are symbolic of the direct access we each have to the Divine, and our innate ability to partner with God in the co-creation of our world and the progression of our souls.

Celebrating Kwan Yin

This book is an offering of love and gratitude to Kwan Yin, Avalokiteshvara, Maha Karuna the Goddess and Buddha of Compassion. I was unaware of the date Kwan Yin's birth is celebrated in the Buddhist tradition until the moment this book was completed. I have now learned that in certain Buddhist traditions her birth is celebrated each year on March 24. Today, the day I send the final version of this book to the publishers is March 23, 2001.

I offer this work to Kwan Yin as a gift and an expression of my gratitude for the wisdom of compassion that she is sharing with humanity, and for the spiritual guidance she provides to me, and many others who are striving to serve the path of compassion in this lifetime.

Foreword

The love that comes from the Creator is unbounded and because of this, there is no limit to the good that can come to those who seek. The potential that lies within us and around us is waiting to unfold and is always available to reveal more and to take us to greater heights. No matter how much we have accomplished or how wonderful something has become there is always the next step, the next lesson, the next development. This is especially true with healing and with Reiki. If we accept this, it makes it possible for us to open to a greater experience of what healing can be.

Karuna Reiki has its roots in Usui and Tibetan Reiki and developed from experimentation with new symbols and attunement techniques. During this process, a knowingness awakened that there was something greater waiting to be uncovered. It was out of this understanding that Karuna Reiki began to manifest here on Earth. I say it in this way because everything that could exist exists now, either in our physical world or on a higher dimension. It is just a matter of seeking something better and being willing to actively follow our inner guidance in order to ground it into our lives.

I did not channel any of the symbols used in Karuna Reiki, but simply began to experiment with non-Usui Reiki symbols that others had channeled. Working with some of my most sensitive students, we allowed ourselves to be guided to the symbols that were best for us and prayed that the Creator would direct our process. Following our guidance, we began to change the way we were doing the attunements. After this, the healing energies began to increase in frequency and strength.

I wondered if we were channeling a new system of Reiki, and after other sensitive healers confirmed it, I slowly came to accept that this was the case. I thanked the Creator and asked what to do next. I was directed to give it a name and the name that came was Karuna. I had not heard of this name before, but found it in a spiritual book and knew it was the right name.

Karuna presents wonderful possibilities for our lives, but to follow this path we must make a choice. In order to fully enjoy the benefits of Karuna, we must be willing to let go of old ways of doing. So often we approach life and its responsibilities with a sense of struggle. Out of fear we assume that we must diligently focus on our worries including being ready to defend ourselves against those who we imagine oppose us. Yet, the reality is that most of our worries are based on false assumptions. They usually never happen, so our energy is dwindled away by needless worry. At other times, because we believe they are real, without knowing it, we end up actually creating what we fear or making existing situations worse. Because of this, a great deal of our time and resources are wasted on worries that never happen or that didn't exist until we acted on our fear. This leaves us in a far less resourceful state and reduces our ability to create the happy, healthy life that we really would like to have. This process has become so habituated into the thinking of many that it is not questioned. It is assumed that mastering this method of doing is the only way to be effective and that there are no alternatives.

Yet, there is a better way. Karuna is an energy that can lift us up to a higher understanding and a healthier way of living our lives. Karuna is an energy that comes from the Creator and also flows through those higher beings that have become liberated from the illusion of the material world. This wonderful energy is filled with compassion for all those that suffer and its intention is to heal. It is all round us and all we need to do is to be attuned to it and invite it in for it to begin its loving work in our lives

Karuna is also a spiritual quality that develops within as we progress on the spiritual path. It creates a gradually developing awareness that we are all one. This feeling of oneness brings with it a power that goes beyond all earthly power. It is not a competitive power or a power that can be used for selfish gain, but a power directed by the Creator. It is the power of love and can be felt in the heart. It heals us and joyously reaches out to help all those around us. It releases all fear, doubt and worry and fills us with hope, peace and grace. It is here to guide us through life and to help us accomplish our spiritual purpose. It lets us know that we are not alone and that we are loved and cared for by the Creator of the Universe. With this comes an open ended feeling of magnificent self worth and a new way of being.

In studying and practicing Karuna Reiki it is my hope that you will keep this higher potential in mind and remain open to the unlimited possibilities that await you within the depths of your own heart.

I thank Laurelle for taking the time to write this wonderful book. It is filled with many techniques and ideas that will help you to use Karuna Reiki more effectively.

May you be deeply blessed.

William Lee Rand

Introduction

As we go about our daily lives, we often remain detached from our awareness of the vastness of creation. We often ignore the unlimited potential we have for creating our own reality through right use of love, energy and intention.

I am offering the information in this book with the hope that it will increase the awareness of a powerful tool for healing and co-creation, Karuna Reiki.

Once we learn how to manifest our own personal visions with tools like Karuna, we can turn our attention to greater things. We then have the potential to unite in groups to hold a common vision for things like peace on earth, environmental healing and prosperity for all people.

Usui Reiki has become relatively well known to people all around the planet as a great healing gift. Many miracles have come out of our use of Usui Reiki, and it has been a great blessing in my life.

Over the years, many people have asked me why we need another energy system like Karuna Reiki when Usui Reiki is so wonderful. It is my feeling that we will continue to need higher frequencies of energy as our species evolves. We live in a limitless Universe, and the healing power of God's love knows no boundaries. As long as there is an appearance of suffering among people and our earth is abused, we must be open to all the healing gifts available to us.

Karuna Reiki was developed by William Rand and the International Center for Reiki Training in Southfield, Michigan. I am honored to serve the ICRT as Director of Teacher Licensing, and I travel worldwide teaching healing techniques including Reiki and Karuna Reiki.

It is important for me to explain that this book is not the "official" word on Karuna Reiki. I am writing this from my personal experiences, and with the help of spiritual guides I am introducing techniques that have been transmitted to me by the energy itself. Over the years I have transcribed these techniques and have used them with wonderful results.

This book in no way replaces Karuna Reiki training, and it is necessary to receive attunements to the energy to be able to fully experience channeling Karuna Reiki. I offer information in this book regarding the contents of a true Karuna Reiki class. I explain the minimum standards and code of ethics required for all Registered Karuna Reiki masters. You will also find details about the Karuna Reiki registration program near the end of the book.

Although I offer much information and many techniques here, I do this only so the limitless nature of spiritual healing can be better understood. This book is meant to be a guide, not a gospel.

I encourage you to always listen to your own heart to find the answers that you seek. Karuna Reiki can be very freeing, as it helps us each to tune in more clearly to our own Divine self and our spiritual guides. The Karuna Reiki energy itself will teach you more than any teacher or book ever will.

Please always listen to the energy and trust your inner knowing ... free yourself to heal!

Om Shanti Gaia . . . Laurelle

Table of Contents

A Soul Healing

I seem to learn my greatest lessons and develop my deepest understanding of healing energies through personal experience. One particularly memorable day Karuna Reiki taught me the true meaning of healing on the soul level.

It was the summer of 1997, the air was crisp and clear and the sounds of a nearby mountain stream were soothing my spirit. I had slipped away for a few moments of quiet introspection at the Karuna Reiki Retreat I was co-facilitating in Colorado that summer. I had just received a most transformational healing thanks to the willing service of my fellow Karuna Reiki Masters and the Karuna Reiki energy.

I have always loved the way in which Reiki brings together the perfect blend of energies into each class, and this carries through to Karuna Reiki classes as well. Sometimes there are karmic healings that need to take place among members of a class, sometimes there is future work to be done together, and other times we are simply brought together to learn new techniques from one another. Whatever the reason, the classes always come together perfectly.

This class was no exception, it brought together exactly the right blend of energies to create the perfect healing environment for each of us.

As I sat by the mountain stream, I perched upon a smooth river rock and dangled my bare feet in the water. The sun was streaming through the trees, sparkling on the rushing water, and a gentle breeze was caressing my skin. This was the perfect place to integrate what had just happened to me.

It had been my turn to receive a healing in our practice sessions. Four beautiful Karuna Reiki Masters gathered around me, joined hands and offered a prayer of intent for my healing. Then they began to channel the Karuna Reiki energy with their voices. As they chanted and sang, I was transported deeper and deeper into the innermost corridors of my being. I was barely aware when the healing channels began to also direct the Karuna Reiki energy with their hands.

Suddenly I felt myself hurtling through time and space at an incredible speed and it seemed as if I were traveling for an eternity. Then the momentum began to slow down, and I was floating on waves of energy. I had no sense of where I was going, I simply knew there was a definite destination and I felt a positive sense of anticipation. I was so very much at one with the currents of energy. I had no form; it was simply the essence of my being that was being transported. Then I began to feel an intense magnetic sensation drawing me closer to my destination.

Next I began to sense a brilliant golden light and I was drawn into this light by the mysterious, magnetic force. I sensed myself merge completely with this light, and instantly felt total and absolute peace. This wasn't simply the calm, peaceful state that I reach in my meditations, or when I do Reiki, this was so very much more. This was soul level peace. I was joy, I was love, I was peace and I was totally home.

As I began to merge more deeply with this golden light, my soul wept tears of bliss from the recognition that this was my soul group. This was my soul group in its entirety...from a timespace near the beginning of creation. We were one light, totally united in absolute love, joy, peace and compassion. I could recognize individual elements of the light, the essence of other beings within my soul group, yet there was no sense of separation. What I was experiencing was ecstasy. I was completely immersed in this experience and felt so safe and secure, I was home.

Then suddenly, without warning, we were blasted apart and I was hurtling all alone into nothingness. I was terrified and overcome with sorrow and loneliness. I was totally isolated from anything familiar, I did not know where I was, or what was happening to me. My soul ached from the sudden sense of disconnection and emptiness.

I began to recognize various levels of my consciousness and from somewhere deep within I heard, "This is the source of our fear of abandonment". The words echoed through my entire being as my consciousness moved closer to my current incarnation.

I gradually became aware of my spiritual body and the words resounded all the way through it. The essence of the words then passed through my mental and emotional bodies and caused my physical body to visibly release deeply seated cellular memory. My personal fear of abandonment was completely healed in this moment because I now recognized this fear for the illusion that it is.

I became fully aware of my surroundings in that cabin in the mountains as I was gently brought back by the soft and loving Karuna Reiki chanting being offered by my friends.

I was dazed by my experience. I still felt the deep ache within my being, yet I felt so very blessed to have experienced absolute peace. I do not long for peace anymore; it is within me and has become a part of my personal truth. I have a deeper understanding that, as part of my purpose on Earth, I am to help others know this as well.

Since that retreat, further work with Karuna Reiki has taught me how to travel back to my soul group at will. I find my healing work evolving as a result of this experience. This work is offering me increasing opportunities to share with individuals who experience deep healing by linking with their soul group. Karuna Reiki continues to help me define, establish and accomplish my Divine purpose in this life.

"Every action of our lives touches
on some chord that will
vibrate in eternity."

Edwin Hubbel Chapin

Karuna Reiki Energy
and Universal Compassion

Karuna Reiki is a healing energy that assists us in awakening to Universal compassion. Many of us are compassionate individuals, however some of us find it more challenging to have compassion for ourselves than for others. This causes us to resist our true unity with the Divine. Karuna helps us shine light into those areas of our being where we hold judgments, criticism and less than loving thoughts about ourselves, others, or world situations. Karuna enhances our ability to see everyone through the eyes of the Divine; as a parent sees a beloved child. When we are able to do this, having compassion is a natural way to be.

Universal or Unconditional Compassion is a stream of consciousness, as is Universal Love. Consciousness itself vibrates only as it is affected by energy. While compassion is the desire to alleviate another's suffering, Universal compassion assists in the alleviation of the illusion of suffering for all beings.

Compassion is a state of consciousness, which when combined with energy, has great transformational power.

In the process of healing, it is important that we learn to fully understand that there is a Divine plan for all of creation, and that we are each a perfect part of that plan.

As we move more clearly into an understanding of the blueprint for our souls, and we use our personal energy every day in creative, positive and loving ways, we align more clearly with the Universal Divine plan.

The energetic essence of the Karuna symbols help us develop an awareness of parts of our personality that have been blocking us, or perhaps causing us to doubt our inner guidance. They also help us to accept, love, and heal those shadows within our personality.

Karuna Reiki is the energy of compassion in action, so it teaches us to have more compassion for others, but also for ourselves. It helps us harmonize the upper and lower chakras, so when we do discern the guidance and wisdom from the Divine, we can move it into the physical realm for manifestation.

Karuna Reiki also has the ability to help us merge our higher self with our lower self, so we can become our Godself in our daily lives.

As we grow more aware of our Divine self, we are more creative and able to act on guidance we receive. We are also empowered to heal co-dependent behaviors, develop reality awareness and become clearer healing channels.

Imagine living on the Earth with all people functioning as their Godself in every moment!

One of the most powerful frequencies in Karuna Reiki helps us develop a complete trust in life, and in our Divine Guidance. This is so important for our growth as individuals and our evolution as a species. Trust in the Divine is absolutely essential, for when we have this trust, there is no fear, and when there is no fear, there can only be peace.

When we are without fear we can follow the guidance we receive, even when it asks us to make sacrifices and let go of things we perceive to be very important to us. We can do this because we trust that the Divine has a bigger and better plan for us than we may be aware of in the moment.

Karuna Reiki can help us understand that we are always precisely where we need to be on our life's path, and to accept all of our experiences and actions as an integral part of who we are. When we learn to accept ourselves with true compassion and love, we begin to honor even those parts of ourselves that we may have felt shame for in the past.

When we walk toward the light, the shadows disappear.

So it is with Karuna Reiki . . . by shining light into the shadows of our being . . . we heal. **Universal Compassion**

Fu hen ji ai

19

"A human being is part of the whole,
called by us "universe", a part limited
in time and space. He experiences himself,
has thoughts and feelings, as something
separate from the rest . . . a kind of optical
delusion of consciousness.

Our task must be to free ourselves by widening
our circles of compassion to embrace all
living creatures and the
whole of nature in its beauty."

Albert Einstein

Qualities of Karuna Reiki Energy

My first impression of Karuna Reiki® was that it is very serious energy. Karuna Reiki goes very deep, gently but quickly. When using or receiving Karuna Reiki I find myself vibrating at a rapidly increasing rate, I feel like I am more light than I am form. The first few times I received a Karuna treatment I felt myself rise out of my body, and I was taken into each of the symbols used.

One repeated occurrence has been that I have seen flashes of traumatic experiences in this life and from other times. They appear before me as if I am looking through a picture window. The image briefly comes into focus so I am clear on what I am seeing, and then a beam of white and gold light pierces the images and shatters them into zillions of pieces, which immediately become pure light. When I have these experiences I have felt and at times have seen physical releases within my body, or the person I was treating. There also have been deep physical and emotional healing experiences.

Karuna Reiki takes many different sensory forms. It can feel like intense heat, wind, ice, electrical impulses, vibration, lightening, humming, or gentle pulsations. Karuna always takes the perfect form whether it is something you feel, see, hear, taste, smell, or simply know.

A beauty of Karuna Reiki is that when major healing issues arise they can be acknowledged, processed and healed in a matter of moments because they are dealt with in their fundamental energetic form. Therefore, when it is appropriate, Karuna Reiki can bring about deep emotional healing without the recipient having to re-live an unpleasant life situation or have an intense emotional experience.

When we receive Karuna Reiki it seems to touch the issue to be healed, lift the energetic essence of the issue to the surface, and then with the recipient's permission it is transformed into pure light and released.

Karuna Reiki and Cellular Healing

Experienced healers often recognize that some clients have more difficulty healing than others. Even when very effective techniques are applied and a client appears to have healed, often their illness recurs. It is as if their bodies revert to old patterns as soon as their stress level escalates. Karuna Reiki can help the body recognize and release old patterns and habits.

During times of extreme stress we develop methods of coping that become encoded into our mental, emotional and physical bodies. Whenever a similar stressful situation arises, the body wants to respond by repeating the earlier patterns. These patterns are known as somatic memories, which unconsciously control our physical body, from the way we walk to the way we breathe, and even to how our injuries heal.

These memories can also be linked to repressed thoughts or emotions. As Karuna Reiki assists us in recognizing these feelings, thoughts or beliefs, we can come to a point where we are ready and willing to release them at the cellular level.

Karuna Reiki allows the body to gently untangle the memories it carries and with each application old patterns are released. Through the essence of Universal compassion, a foundation for new, healthy patterns is created.

Although Karuna facilitates healing, it does not do the healing. Karuna energy simply assists by reflecting information to the body's systems and allows healing to take place from within the person.

Because Karuna Reiki can facilitate the healing of cellular memory, there are times that dramatic physical changes take place. One personal experience I had was the healing of a scar on my leg that had been there for 30 years.

After working with Karuna I began to randomly notice that there were bruises that would appear on my leg. I could never remember bumping my leg, or any physical cause for the bruises. Then one day I realized that whenever a bruise appeared, I had either just given a Karuna treatment or taught a Karuna class.

I began to watch that leg very closely, and what I realized was the energy was releasing cellular memory of the injury and the release was so intense that it produced minor bruising. When the bruise healed, the area underneath was completely healed and there was no evidence of the scar.

In the same way that Karuna can help heal physical evidence of cellular memory, it can also help us re-pattern on the mental and emotional levels. This helps us create healthier responses for our life situations.

Our Evolving Subtle Energy System

To better understand how Karuna Reiki is able to create such powerful healing effects it is helpful to know a little about the transpersonal chakras that Karuna Reiki chooses to activate and permeate.

Because there are many books that explain the basic chakra system, I will not address the 7 basic chakras. If you wish to read more about them I recommend Anodea Judith's book, "_Wheels of Life_".

In order for our body to be able to integrate the higher frequency healing rays that are being anchored on the planet at this time, our subtle energy system must be able to hold more light than in the past.

The activation of transpersonal chakras, such as the stellar gateway, soul star, causal chakra, etheric heart, earth star and Gaia gateway is vital. This is, in part, what Karuna Reiki is doing for us. It is helping our transpersonal energy system become more fully activated. Please refer to the diagram in this section for the positioning of these chakras.

The stellar gateway and soul star chakras are portals through which very high frequency light can enter our etheric field. The stellar gateway is like a spiritual barometer that measures the intensity of light our field can hold. The soul star is the filter through which the light is measured and flows. The soul star also facilitates access to our personal library within the akashic records.

The causal chakra is the center that accepts the "dosages" of light that the upper two chakras deliver, and it assists in higher activations of the crown, brow and throat chakras.

The ascending heart and sacred heart chakras house the essence of Universal Compassion and Universal Love. They create a triad via an etheric link with the heart chakra.

There is a holographic projection of the link between these three centers held in the subtle energy field. This hologram is known as the etheric heart. Its purpose is to facilitate communication via the language of light between our soul, the Universal Heart, and the Universal Mind.

Although the diagram depicts the etheric heart in what appears to be a fixed position in our subtle energy field, it is not stationary. We are dealing with a multidimensional light-form that is in constant motion: pulsing in and out of various layers and positions within our etheric field.

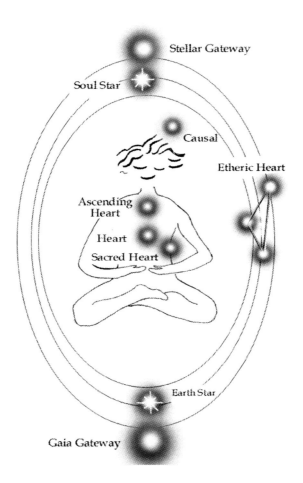

When giving a Karuna Reiki treatment, an awareness that both your energy system and the client's are affected in the same way is helpful. As we are anchoring these higher frequencies, our energy bodies are able to speak to one another through the language of light. Through this interaction between practitioner and client, Karuna Reiki receives the "information" that it needs.

Please keep in mind that it is _not_ necessary to have an intellectual understanding of the transpersonal chakra system, or even the basic chakras in order to work with Karuna Reiki. I only give this brief explanation here because it seems to help us better understand _how_ Karuna functions differently than many other healing rays. This can partially explain some of the phenomenal results we see so often with Karuna Reiki.

Remember, this energy knows exactly what to do in every situation, and it knows precisely how to do it. I find it a great honor to facilitate healing by simply being a vehicle for this infinitely wise, Divinely powerful, energy to flow through.

If you have an interest in exploring the transpersonal system from an experiential level I would recommend working with Karuna Reiki and the following crystals/gemstones.

Kyanite (blue or green), white selenite, golden selenite, moldavite, peridot, tanzanite, kunzite, rose optical calcite, aquamarine, aqua aura, and rutilated topaz.

Crystals and Gemstones
Tools for Exploration

You will find reference to crystals in the sections of this book on symbols and on our subtle energy system.

There are no absolute rules in working with crystals. They are tools for enhancing our exploration and ability to discern the vibrations of Karuna Reiki energy.

The stones listed in each section help to intensify specific qualities of Karuna Reiki energy. For example when the stones listed in the previous section are charged with Karuna Reiki, holding them or meditating with them can help us sense the different transpersonal energy centers. Those listed in the symbols section can help us connect more clearly with the unique vibration of each symbol.

It is always a good idea to cleanse crystals and stones before you work with them. There are many ways to do this. You can cleanse crystals by placing them in direct sunlight for several hours, placing them in a dish of sea salt, smudging with sage or cedar smoke, burying them in the earth, or channeling the Usui power symbol into them with the intention of lifting anything less than light out of the crystal and purifying it.

Charging crystals is very simple, you can draw an image of the symbol(s) you want to work with over the stone and channel energy into it. Another way is to visualize the symbol(s) floating in a ball of light above your head. Inhale imagine you are breathing in through the crown of your head. Your in-breath will contain the essence of the symbol(s). Hold the crystal in your hands and exhale with all your power into the crystal intending that the stone will retain the healing energies and carry the essence of the symbols.

When working with crystals as indicated in this book, the intention is not to do bodywork on self or others. Crystal healing is an entire modality in itself and deserves serious and thorough study. The intention for the use of crystals as described here is to help the practitioner develop a deeper understanding of the nature of Karuna energy.

"Hands of invisible spirits
touch the strings of that
mysterious instrument,
the soul."

Longfellow

Discerning Our Spiritual Guidance

One of the many wonderful characteristics of Karuna Reiki is its inherent potential to increase our ability to recognize and discern spiritual guidance. This can be a very valuable tool for our growth. Our spiritual guides assist us in lightening the path of our soul's progression. They help us better understand how to stay focused on our purpose in this life. I have also learned that spiritual guides can be instrumental in the development of new, healing techniques and modalities.

Karuna Reiki is a powerful tool for discerning Divine Guidance. We all have intuitive abilities, which are developed to varying degrees. Intuition is one of our greatest gifts. When we listen and act upon our intuitive knowing, we grow stronger spiritually. When we ignore this guidance … well that's a different story.

What is Divine Guidance? When I speak of Divine Guidance, I mean the inspiration from the mind of God that is available to each of us. This wisdom helps us accomplish our lifetime purpose. This is the same type of inspiration that guides Reiki energies. It is infinitely wise and knows exactly what is best for us.

Divine Guidance is just that, guidance. We are never forced to follow it because we do have free will. We also do not have to even listen. Guidance comes to us in different forms, sometimes as inspiration, and at other times it brings us messages of caution: perhaps to slow down, or pursue a totally different direction.

How many times have you had an intuitive feeling that you should not follow through with a certain action or particular project, yet you have ignored your inner knowing? What happens when you continue to try to move forward? Does it feel a little like struggling to push a boulder uphill? It's similar to watching a traffic light ahead of you turn yellow, and responding by pounding the accelerator to the floor. The result is you run a red light and life may become unpleasant in that moment.

I have learned that when I feel those twinges of intuition, life is much easier if I listen and follow the advice I am receiving.

Conversely, the intuitive guidance that prompts us to move forward or heightens our awareness of new opportunities is offered to us as well. When we follow that inner knowing, even when we don't know why, we are rarely disappointed.

If you wish to be able to clearly hear, listen and discern the guidance available to you, Karuna Reiki can help.

I have always felt quite in tune with my intuition, but there were so many times that I would wonder, am I just imagining this? I would ask myself how I could be absolutely certain that the guidance I was receiving was indeed Divine and not my imagination, or some other energy trying to distract me from my path. It was not until I studied and began regular practice of Karuna Reiki that I became totally confident in my ability to discern the guidance I was receiving.

So how has Karuna Reiki helped me tune in more clearly and trust this guidance? First of all one of the immediate experiences I had was an increased awareness of the vast amount of spiritual help available to us. I was introduced to guides, angels and Masters that I never knew existed before Karuna. This happens to many people who study this wonderful healing energy because the vibrational frequency of Karuna Reiki is so high. It takes us spiritually to a very special place.

There is a realm that blends Heaven and Earth, where Truth and Wisdom reside. In this realm we access our limitless potential as Divine beings. This blending place offers a wealth of spiritual knowledge, creative inspiration, blessings and guiding energies that assist us on the path of our soul's progression.

You can think of this as a "blending place" as a realm where mortals come together with spiritual and angelic beings. In order for us to exist in the physical dimension, we must be able to maintain a certain density in our vibration. In order for the guides to access the frequencies that contain higher forms of spiritual wisdom and inspiration, they must be able to maintain their vibration at a higher level.

Spiritual beings are capable of manifesting in the physical, and have done so in places like Medjugore where the Divine Mother has appeared to many. There have been manifestations like this in many places around the world. However, in order for this to happen, these ascended beings must slow their vibration so that they are visible in our third dimensional plane of life.

The Karuna Reiki blending point is a realm where we can meet our guides, and maintain a higher frequency. In this place wonderful things can happen as we communicate more clearly with the angels, masters and guides. Once we experience this type of connection with the guides, and we know how it feels to receive this guidance, we no longer need to question the wisdom we receive on a daily basis. This is because the feeling, the knowing, and resonance we experience, we never forget. Then when we sense it in our daily life we know, without a doubt that a high form of guidance is being offered to us.

I worked regularly with the Karuna symbols in meditation to help myself grow in this area. The energy of the symbols helps us deal with previous trauma and to heal on the cellular level. They help us work with the guides to heal karmic issues and to strengthen the light around us. Because like attracts like, as our light becomes brighter and clearer. We then attract stronger light from the guides, as well as friends, family and colleagues. This is in part why we often find our relationships changing as we grow spiritually.

The guidance I have received with the help of Karuna Reiki has assisted me in making some of the most difficult decisions of my life because it has increased my ability to listen and to act upon my guidance.

In the past few years I have been rebirthing myself. I have had to let go of friends and even distance myself from family members who were not in harmony with the spiritual intensity that flows through me. I was guided to divorce after 20 years of marriage, move, and create a totally new form of expressing my purpose through my work.

I have done this while expressing only love to those I have been guided to release into my past, and holding that love in my heart even when some could not continue to hold love for me. Although at times this has been a painful process, it has taught me the meaning of compassion on a higher level than ever before.

I have "sacrificed" a lot that was dear to me because I knew I must do so in order to fulfill my mission in this life. I am at peace with that because Karuna Reiki is helping me trust and grow. I also realize that what I once felt was a sacrifice was actually my putting Universal Compassion into action in my life. I now see the "sacrifices" as joyous blessings.

At one point in my re-birthing process I was "asked" by my guides to change my name. To me, this was a powerful expression of letting go of old forms. When I was guided to change my name to Laurelle Shanti Gaia, because my purpose is to assist in the manifestation of peace on Earth (Shanti means peace and Gaia is the living being that is our Mother Earth), I had to reach deep into my reserve of trust. I was able to do all of this, and maintain peace in my heart because I know that the Divine has a greater plan than I am able to see at times.

I have become very focused on my purpose for being on this planet, and that is to raise the peace vibration through a variety of methods and to teach and empower others to do this as well. I have recognized this "calling" since I was a child, yet I didn't understand it intellectually then.

Since I have embraced Karuna Reiki in my life I have emerged from that land of forgotten purpose. I am remembering who I am, why I am here; and I am being guided every step of the way.

If you find yourself at a point in your life where you feel it is time that you awaken fully to your potential and purpose for this lifetime. If you desire to understand what your personal mission is and how you are to express it, you may find the power contained within Karuna Reiki energy to be a tool to help you in your discovery. Karuna can help you find peace and trust in your own Divine Guidance.

"The best and most beautiful things
in the world cannot be seen,
nor touched . . .
but are felt in the heart."

Helen Keller

Recognizing Our Spiritual Guides

One thing that is important for us to know is that guides can come to us in a limitless number of forms, or with no form at all. Sometimes guides appear as a human, animal, angel, or light being. At other times guides may be simply swirling masses of energy or color that we sense or see in our mind's eye.

I have guides that communicate with me through sensations in my body. For example when feeling a particular type of tingling around my shoulders and arms, I have come to know that is a signal one of my guides is working with me to teach me new ways to direct energy. Other guides communicate through telepathic messages, sound, scent or by initiating a strong sense of inner _knowing_ within me.

The guides who work with Karuna Reiki˚ are highly evolved. I remember one experience when a new guide introduced itself in one of the classes I was teaching. This was a being that no one in the class had an intellectual knowledge of at the time, but throughout the class we were given clues to help us learn the identity of this spiritual master, Avalokiteshvara. Avalokiteshvara is known in Buddhism as Maha (Great) Karuna (Compassion) and is often depicted in artwork as a being with many arms. Avalokiteshvara is an incarnation of Kwan Yin, the Chinese Goddess of compassion and mercy.

Since those of us in the class had little or no knowledge of Buddhism, it was a very intriguing experience. It is important to know that the guides that work with Karuna Reiki are not exclusively related to the Buddhist religion, or any other religion in particular. Guides such as Jesus, Mother Mary, Mother Teresa, Krishna, Gandhi, Archangel's Michael and Gabriel, etc. have all been reported as beings who are guiding us in our use of Karuna Reiki

Over the years guides who come to me have been of vastly different vibrations. In this past year, as the earth healing work has evolved, Maha Chohan has come to assist.

His first contact with me was during one of my few treasured moments at home. I am blessed to live in a very rural area of the Colorado in the mountains, far from the electromagnetic and disruptive energetic interferences that are so common in the city. This creates an environment that is very conducive to traveling between the veils, asking for and receiving spiritual guidance. However, I have given my guides permission to spontaneously contact me when there is a need to transmit information through my writings.

I am sharing this particular experience with you because at first I did not know what was happening to me, and perhaps if anything similar happens to you, remembering this story will help you relax into the experience.

I had gone to bed and was reading. Suddenly I began to feel a sensation almost as if I couldn't breath, I felt intense pressure in every part of my body. I didn't actually feel pain, just intense pressure from the *inside* of my body moving outward. Shudders of energy repeatedly went through my body, like shock waves, causing a minor-convulsive response. I didn't know what was happening and I was beginning to feel fearful. I told Michael what I was experiencing, and he immediately began to pray and channel healing energy. In just moments I was rising up as if someone had lifted me up and stood me on my feet. I was walking to the computer and before I knew it, a message from Maha Chohan had appeared on the screen before me.

His vibration is so very intense I was experiencing a challenge in physically being able to integrate the energy. I have found that Karuna Reiki and the Infinite Light techniques are absolutely necessary for my body to be able to hold the intensity of his vibration.

Through the use of healing energies and prayer we are now working together more effectively. He has explained to me that those people who are receiving these transmissions are now accepting them in a form that is more intense than has been known to humanity in the past. We are able to receive them now because of systems like Karuna Reiki and other high frequency forms of healing light that facilitate our integration of the transmitted energies and the ultimate transcription of them.

Angelic Assistance

One of the things that I have learned, with the assistance of Karuna Reiki, is how to work with the Archangel Realms. I found that working with the Archangels, and specifically through our personal realm of incarnation, we are offered powerful assistance on the path of our soul's progression. I have since incorporated this knowledge into the long distance healing work I do to assist with soul profiling/clearing, crystalline soul light activation, and theta level healing.

Throughout time, and through many sacred traditions there has been much taught about the angelic hierarchy. What I am introducing here are ways to work with the Archangel realms, Divine temples and Karuna Reiki to assist in enhancing your awareness of the spiritual guidance available. In the techniques section, you will find specific methods of using Karuna energy to facilitate working with spiritual guides.

I would like to introduce you to some very basic information regarding the Archangel Realms that you may find helpful.

When using Karuna Reiki, I work primarily with the following nine Archangel realms:

Realm and Divine Temple	Divine Purpose	Colors and Chakra	Crystals
Auriel Compassion	Universal compassion, Nature, Earth	**Ruby Red/Forest Green** Base	Ruby/Malachite Quantum*/Moss Agate
Zadkiel Creation	Manifestation, visualization, Creativity	**Saffron/Violet** Sacral	Rhodocrosite/Orange and Purple Sapphire/Vanadinite
Michael Truth	Strength, protection, truth, Balance of light	**Cobalt Blue/Yellow** Solar Plexus	Azurite/Citrine/Pearl Amber/Tanzanite
Raphael Love	Healing, love, Emotional experience	**Iridescent Green/Pink** Heart	Pink Kunzite/Muscovite Chrysoprase/Apophylite
Alteal Peace	Peace, evolution, Dimensional awareness	**Aqua/Gold/Cream** Ascending Heart	Aquamarine/Aqua Aura Alabaster/Calcite (all colors)
Gabriel Knowledge	Teaching, sound, Communication, alchemy	**Lt.Blue/Emerald Green** Throat	Blue Calcite/Emerald Moldavite/Golden Labradorite
Zophkiel Beauty/Sight	Beauty, artistic expression, Divine law and order	**Indigo/Crimson** Brow	Lapis/Rubelite Pink Tourmaline
Camiel Light	Light, power, prayer, energy	**Violet/Gold** Crown	Ametrine/Charoite Sugilite/Golden Selenite
Haniel Purpose	Magnificence, Aligning with Divine Power/Purpose	**Crimson/White** Soul Star	White Selenite, Herkimer, Crimson Elbaite

There may be as many interpretations of the angelic realms as there are schools of religious or spiritual teachings. The information presented here is a guide for working with Karuna Reiki and the Archangels.

I have listed the nine primary Archangel realms that assist us in developing certain spiritual characteristics. Invoking assistance from these realms while accessing Karuna Reiki is a powerful way to accelerate healing and spiritual growth. Sometimes this type of rapid growth can bring opportunities in rather harsh forms. I have found that by working with the Archangel realms and the Divine temples these growth opportunities are presented to us more gently than without invoking this assistance.

As an example of how to work with this information let's focus on the Archangel Realm of Auriel:

Realm and Divine Temple	Divine Purpose	Colors and Chakra	Crystals
Auriel Compassion	Universal compassion, Nature, Earth	Ruby Red/Forest Green Base	Ruby/Malachite Quantum*/Moss Agate

The purpose of this realm is to help humanity develop a true sense of Universal Compassion and a deeper soul level connection with the nature kingdom and our earth. By invoking assistance from this realm and meditating in the Divine Temple of Compassion after activating Karuna Reiki we can learn a great deal. We also have an opportunity to truly *know* and express Universal Compassion by experiencing the energetic essence it holds.

The colors and crystals are also tools that can assist in our connection to this realm and temple.

In the symbols section of this book entitled "Karuna Symbols and our Spiritual Guides" I offer suggestions regarding how to use the Karuna energies that facilitate the invocation of the primary Archangel realms, and aid in traveling to the related Divine temples.

Physical Considerations

We all have the ability to develop finely tuned spiritual perception and to communicate with our guides. In addition to using Karuna Reiki to increase your vibratory rate there are some physical preparations that are helpful.

Nourishing our body with "high frequency foods" supports our communication with our guides. These are foods that are most often easier to digest, contain no synthetic chemicals, and are prepared with simplicity so they remain as close as possible to their natural form.

Foods such as fresh vegetables, fruits and grains hold the highest vibration. Seafood and poultry hold the next highest vibration. Consuming meat from animals with hooves, such as beef, pork, venison, etc. slows metabolism and thus lowers our vibration.

Our consumption of pure water is also very important. Water helps to conduct energy and facilitates spiritual communication while helping to integrate higher frequencies with greater ease.

Water used in a bath is beneficial also. Water is the element of the second chakra and has a direct cleansing and balancing effect on the emotional body. When our emotional body is clear, our pathway to our mental body is more open. Spiritual guides communicate with us by sending information from our spiritual connection with them into our mental body so that we can bring their wisdom into our conscious awareness.

Bathing with sea salt, or Epsom salt and baking soda is very helpful in preparing for spiritual communication. Another combination, which is less drying and you may prefer is mixing one cup of the salts with one cup of vinegar. (Do not add baking soda if you use the vinegar). After either of these baths it is advisable to rinse off in the shower to remove any residue from your skin.

Bathing prior to doing any type of spiritual work helps to clear our entire subtle energy field and assists in our ability to hear and discern guidance from the spiritual realms.

Massaging or applying light pressure to specific parts of the body can also be helpful. I find that applying gentle pressure and repetitively pressing in and releasing the point where our ribs meet is helpful. This is a light pumping action.

Next I use the same technique and then "thump" the ascending heart chakra with my fingers. I then place my index and fire (middle) finger on my third eye and massage gently in clockwise circles. The next step, using the same fingers, is to lightly press in the area beneath the causal chakra , which is located on the crown of the head, at the back and slightly to the left of the middle.

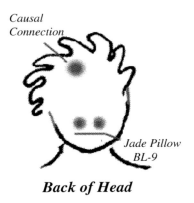

Causal Connection

Jade Pillow BL-9

Back of Head

I then massage the back of the head along the bladder meridian. There are two points there known as Yuzhen, Jade Pillow or BL9. These points are approximately 2 ½ inches above the neck hairline. They are massaged simultaneously.

Additionally we have two pathways in our body known as functioning and governing channels. The functioning channel carries energy up the front of our body to the tip of our tongue. This channel is often also referred to as the conception meridian. The governing channel carries energy up the spine, over the crown of the head to the roof of the mouth.

When these two meridians are joined, our spiritual sensitivity is increased. This sensitivity can come in the form of intuition, clairvoyant sight, inner knowing or clairaudience.

There is an exercise that can facilitate connecting the functioning and governing channels. It is a simple contraction of the perineum, which is also know as the Hui Yin point. The Hui Yin is located between the anus and the genitals. Contraction of this point is also an exercise performed to prepare for childbirth and is known as Kagel contractions. Repetitively contracting and releasing this point stimulates our spiritual and physical vision centers.

When placing the tip of the tongue on the roof of the mouth, resting behind the front teeth and contracting the Hui Yin, an energy circuit is created connecting these two channels. If you feel a slight sensation between your eyes, you are doing this exercise correctly.

A visualization that I find helpful in bringing spiritual messages into my conscious mind is illustrated and described here:

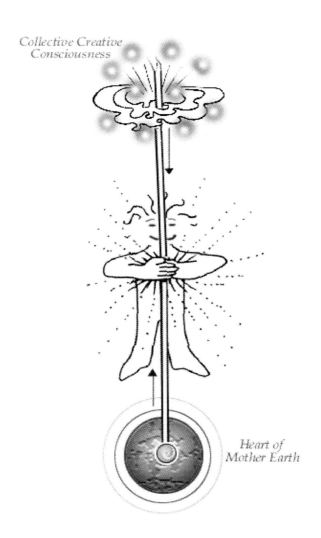

Collective Creative
Consciousness

Heart of
Mother Earth

"Imagine the Collective Creative Consciousness as a sea of light above you. See a golden ribbon of light streaming down from this into the crown of your head. This golden ribbon contains the pure essence of Infinite Love from the Heart of God and Infinite Light from the Mind of God.

Allow Infinite Love and Light to enter into the crown of your head as it slowly moves down through your body. Your body is filling with magnificent golden liquid light.

All stress is leaving your body and your mind is becoming calm. Infinite Light and Infinite Love are permeating every atom and every cell of who you are. Allow yourself to feel these sensations.

The golden ribbon flows down your legs, out your feet and down into the earth. Imagine this golden ribbon flowing through the various layers of the earth, all the way to the crystalline core at the heart of Mother Earth.

Feel your connection to the earth. You are anchoring the highest and most holy spiritual energies into the heart of the earth in this very moment. You are a pillar of light.

Now feel a pulsation of warm nurturing energy from the heart of Mother Earth as it travels back up that ribbon of light, and into your body. This sublime energy streams out the crown of your head and flows into the Heart and Mind of God.

Feel the Love of the Earth and the Love of God pulsating within your being. Feel your connection to all there is. In this connected state, voice a sacred intention that you are open to receive guidance from the Masters, angels and spiritual beings who are available to assist you. Invoke their presence and welcome them".

This visualization can be done in just a few moments and is facilitated by the use of Karuna Reiki energy.

Inviting Assistance

As we desire to access more of the wisdom our guides have to share with us, we must remember to ask for their help and invoke their presence. They will not interfere. They must be invited or given permission to help us.

There is a prayer that comes from the work of the Master Djwhal Khul and Alice Bailey known as the Great Invocation. This is a very powerful prayer that will invoke the presence and assistance of the Ascended Masters and other enlightened beings. I start my day with this invocation.

The Great Invocation

"From the point of Light within the Mind of God

Let light stream forth into the minds of men.

Let Light descend on Earth

From the point of Love within the Heart of God

Let love stream forth into the hearts of men

May Christ return to Earth

From the center where the Will of God is known

Let purpose guide the lower wills of men

The purpose which the Masters know and serve.

From the center which we call the race of men

Let the Plan of Love and Light work out.

And may it seal the door where evil dwells

Let Light and Love and Power restore the Plan on Earth"

And So It Is

I recite the Great Invocation daily to invite the Masters into my life. In addition I also offer the following prayer, which invokes gentle guidance:

"I call upon my guardians and angels of light to help me on this day.

I give thanks for my awareness, discernment and right use of the wisdom they share with me.

I give thanks for their help as together we lighten the path of my soul's progression."

And So It Is

As your guides work with you, remain open to the many forms in which they manifest and the unlimited ways they communicate and can assist you. Use Karuna Reiki' to take you to the blending place where we are able to commune with these magnificent beings of light.

When you find yourself in this special place between the veils always remember to ... Listen!

Listening to our heart,
finding out who we are, is not simple.

It takes time for the chatter to quiet down.

In the silence of "not doing"
we begin to know what we feel.

If we listen and hear what is being offered,
then anything in life can be our guide.

Listen

~ Author Unknown ~

Mother Teresa's Call for Compassionate Action

The following is adapted from an article that I wrote for an issue of *Reiki News*. It seems appropriate to share it with you because it illustrates how guides sometimes only give us glimpses of their presence. Often our guides gradually reveal themselves to us, and this story is an example of that process.

In early February I awoke to a record snowfall at my home in Louisville, Kentucky. It was beautiful and a bit of a novelty for us to be snowed in for several hours. However, I was scheduled to begin teaching a Karuna Reiki® class that morning. The roads were closed and I had people from out of town snowed in waiting for class. It was nice though, the normal pre-class rush that often takes place on the first day just didn't happen. I was able to enjoy the morning so fully. Soon the sun began to clear the roads and we were able to start class in the early afternoon. Little did we know that the purity and peace the snow brought with it was a prelude to the great blessing we were to receive.

This was an interesting class in many ways, but an especially wonderful thing happened for our group. Over the course of three days we became gradually aware of a beautiful energetic presence. It was a new Master energy we hadn't felt before. It was a feminine energy, very soft, extremely compassionate, yet very focused and powerful. At first she appeared as simply a sentient experience. Then a most radiant, shimmering, pale blue light began to form. Soon we became aware that this was the compassionate presence of Mother Teresa.

This awareness brought tears to my eyes, and a deep feeling of humility and gratitude. I had admired Mother Teresa for many years, and have borrowed some of her quotes to help motivate others and myself. One of my favorites is:

"There is a Light in this world...
a healing spirit much stronger than any darkness we may encounter.

We sometimes lose sight of this force...
where there is suffering, too much pain.

And suddenly the spirit will emerge... through the lives of ordinary people
and answer in extraordinary ways."

Since the class I have prayed and meditated about this. It seemed too soon after her transition to experience Mother Teresa's energy in this way. However, others who have experience with Karuna Reiki* have been sensing her presence in their work as well. I shared our experience with William Rand and he reminded me that she had made her transition during our Karuna Reiki retreat in Michigan the past September, and that he had seen her standing with Jesus.

In my meditations she is asking that we continue working to unite the Reiki community, and that we focus on our mission of expressing our compassion through action. That is what she tried to teach us. Having compassion is the first step, but taking action on that compassion is another story. Karuna means compassionate action.

One thing that Karuna Reiki has done for me personally, and very consistently, is to increase my awareness of the spiritual guidance available to me for my work and my life. I am now guided by Master energies that I had never been aware of before, they help in many ways.

When we use the very fine vibrational frequencies associated with Karuna Reiki , we increase our personal vibration so that we can hold higher frequencies of light for longer periods of time. This makes it easier for spiritual beings that exist at even higher levels to reach us and communicate ways we can work together to help our planet awaken to healing.

Karuna Reiki Masters are aligning with other healing practitioners and networking to focus healing energy on world crisis situations. The Karuna Reiki system contains within it symbols to help us access frequencies to increase the vibration of peace on the planet, and to assist the Earth in her healing.

Mother Teresa's guidance has inspired me to expand services available through my wellness center, find new ways to share peace work and to find ways to make Reiki and healing accessible to more people. As long as I am receiving guidance regarding more ways to share love and compassion, I will listen and I will act upon the guidance that feels right within my heart. Mother Teresa's guidance continues in many positive ways.

Please take a moment to read a more thought provoking quotations from Mother Teresa:

"In the developed countries there is a poverty of intimacy, a poverty of spirit, of loneliness, of lack of love. There is no greater sickness in the world today than that one."

"When a poor person dies of hunger, it has not happened because God did not take care of him or her. It has happened because neither you nor I wanted to give that person what he or she needed."

I hope some of these words of wisdom touch your heart as they have mine. Mother Teresa made a powerful, positive impact on millions of people in her life. She did this by acting on a call to service she heard those many years ago. She answered that call and walked her path with much love offering acts of kindness to those most in need. Each of us has a purpose for being on this planet. When we know that purpose we have the opportunity to manifest it.

When we shine our light brightly upon our path we will always be shown the way.

Historical Origins of Karuna Reiki

Karuna Reiki is a system of healing that has evolved out of the Usui Reiki system, which is believed to have been discovered in 1914 by Mikao Usui on the holy mountain of Kurama near Kyoto, Japan.

When translated from Sanskrit, Karuna means compassionate action accompanied by wisdom. The combination of the energetic essence of Karuna and Reiki, which is spiritually guided life force energy, births a new, deep, powerful healing form for our world.

Although Karuna Reiki was not part of the system of Reiki that was originated in Japan by Usui Sensei, I feel that it is an evolution of Usui Reiki that has come forth as a direct expression of the expansion of the Reiki energy itself.

There were over a million people practicing Usui Reiki on the planet when we moved into the new millennium. Those people who practice diligently and apply Reiki to all aspects of their lives are continuously receiving guidance directly from the Reiki energy regarding new ways to use it. It is not uncommon for new symbols or keys to higher frequencies of the healing rays to be given to dedicated Reiki practitioners.

Over a period of several years contemporary Reiki Masters Marcy Miller, Kellie-Ray Marine, Catherine Mills-Bellamont, Marla Abraham, and Pat Courtney, each received symbols as part of their healing work. When symbols come to us they are often given to us as personal healing tools. Sometimes they are to be shared with other healers. The Karuna Reiki symbols were channeled with names and specific instructions for drawing them. Very basic uses for the symbols were also received at the time they were transmitted to the individuals who brought them into this third dimension.

The International Center for Reiki Training (ICRT) is an organization that offers professional Reiki training programs, teaching aids for Reiki Masters, and healing tools for Reiki practitioners. The ICRT also assists the international Reiki community through dissemination of information.

As a result of the services offered by the ICRT, people from all around the world send healing symbols to the Center in Michigan. William Rand, president of the ICRT, was presented with many such symbols, and among them were symbols that have since become part of the Karuna Reiki system.

William worked with the symbols through practice, prayer and meditation, and was ultimately guided to develop the original system known as Karuna Reiki. Through the years William, myself and other teachers have worked with these energies and learned much more about the symbols, the energy and ways to use them to enhance life.

Karuna Reiki has taught me a great deal about advanced levels of healing, which is why I am writing this book. It is my prayer that what I share here will help this powerful healing energy to be better understood and incorporated into the healing evolution on our planet in greater ways.

"I want to know how God
created this world."

Albert Einstein

Spiritual Origins of Karuna Reiki˚

Dimensional Links

The more I use Karuna Reiki, the more I recognize that it is somehow facilitating an inter-dimensional flow of energies. By this I mean it is allowing the practitioner to activate soul memory of healing technologies from ancient times, and to link through the dimensions to bring them into the current time space that we know to be third dimensional reality.

Through the use of Karuna Reiki, we have the opportunity to expand our concept of reality. It is so easy to become focused on our daily lives in the third dimension and believe that is all there is; or think it is the only thing of importance. Sometimes it seems as if we are afraid to let ourselves believe in the vastness of creation.

We can begin to understand the idea of inter-dimensional realities, or other planes of existence; if, for a moment, we forget everything we think we know about linear time and imagine that perhaps time is actually a continuum.

Imagine time as a continuous flow of energy that contains all the events that have ever happened, are happening in this moment, or will ever happen. If this is so, then we can also imagine being able to train our mind to blend with our higher consciousness, and with the proper tools, link in with past and future events and cultures.

As strange as this may seem, it might be one explanation for past life memory, as well as how and why some of us are tapping into Lemurian, Atlantean, Egyptian and Biblical healing techniques and systems. This is happening to many healers as they raise their vibration and release their fears of the unknown and travel into these other dimensions or planes of consciousness, tapping into the time continuum.

It is very common for new Karuna Reiki practitioners to receive glimpses of Biblical or Egyptian times, including memories or visions of healing chambers inside the pyramids, healing oils and rituals. It is my intuitive sense that the reason these times are the first to be recalled is that the energy of those times is denser than the Atlantean and Lemurian times.

Lemurian's were both physical and etheric beings and thus the energy of their time is of a higher vibration than the Atlantean's and ancient Egyptian's. As we work with Karuna Reiki and other high vibrational healing technologies, our vibration raises and we are able to tap into the crystal temples of Atlantis, and the rainbow crystalline energy of the Lemurian temples and chambers.

Something that has come very clear to me as I work with Karuna is that the power of the group in healing is nothing short of phenomenal. A group is truly powerful when all of the people serving as instruments for healing energy to flow through can truly set their personalities and egos aside. When all members of a group come together with clear intention and pure hearts, miracles happen.

In Lemuria telepathic abilities were very highly developed among the leaders and the power of group energy was truly understood. It was through a group of Lemurian's who had highly evolved telepathic abilities, holding a common vision, and channeling specific frequencies of energy; that buildings, temples, pyramids, etc. were constructed. The Lemurian's manifested what they needed using prayer, focused intention, collective vision and energy.

Knowing these things about Lemuria helps explain to me why so much of what were are being guided to do now involves holding a common vision, channeling energy, and waiting until the vision manifests.

Oneness - A Lemurian Explanation

There is a Lemurian guide who works with me, and a group of friends. Her name is Lamaya. I had never been aware of her until one day this particular group gathered, prayed, meditated and sent energy together. Lamaya came to us at that time and explained the concept of "adamantine particles of light". She said that we are all truly one, and that our souls are made of an infinite number of light particles. These particles of light hold the essence of every soul, and therefore the memories that they hold. These are the adamantine particles of light.

She laughed as she explained why so many people sense that they were Cleopatra, Edgar Cayce, or witnessed the crucifixion of Jesus. She explained that this is because it is true! Our soul blueprint, or personal akashic record, holds the essence of every single experience of every incarnate and non-incarnate soul. Therefore we are truly one with all there is.

As I am writing this, I can't help but wonder if this is too "out there" for some of you reading this. However, I have a very strong sense that it is important to introduce these concepts here. You don't have to embrace this information as your truth, but I ask that you consider it as a possibility.

Since I was a very young child I have had an inner knowing that what I have described here is true to me, but I didn't understand how it could be. Living in a logical, analytical world it is very difficult to accept. However, since the introduction of Karuna Reiki into my life, I am remembering more every day of the limitless nature of creation, and I am learning to be open to all possibilities.

"Prayer is not verbal.
It is from the heart.
To merge into the heart is prayer."

Sri Ramana Maharishi

Visualization and Prayer

The term visualization may be one of the most misunderstood terms used today. For some people the very thought of visualizing something creates fear and causes them to shut down.

Visualization is simply *practical imagination*. I learned long ago; "What the mind can conceive, and the heart can believe, you can achieve."

Greg Braden says something similar in his book *The Isaiah Effect* "It is the powerful combination of the alignment of your thoughts in your mind, with the emotion in your bodies, which result in the feeling in your heart."

People who don't think they can visualize can be guided in a very simple meditation to close their eyes and imagine that they are standing at their front door. By asking them which direction they are facing; what they feel, sense or see; they are usually amazed at how easy it is to visualize. It is simple to imagine what you *feel* like standing outside your front door.

Prayer is the act of speaking with the Divine from that quiet space, deep inside ourselves where we can sense the heartbeat of our soul. This is a place of power from which to state our sacred intentions and hold our visions.

Mystics have believed in the power of prayer since ancient times. It is through prayer, visualization, affirmation, and experiencing or feeling the essence of what we are praying for that causes miracles and blessings to manifest in our lives. These are the tools of creation.

Accessing our Divine power to create involves holding a vision of what we wish to create, combined with affirmation, and sacred intention stated in prayer.

One of the keys here is holding the vision. By this I mean we imagine what it *looks* like and what it *feels* like to have what we desire. I often ask students, "What is the essence of what you want to create in your life? What qualities will it bring with it? How will it change your life?"

It might go something like this.

"I want a better job."

"When you get that better job, what will you have that you don't have now?"

"More money and less stress."

"What does it feel like to have more money and less stress? What does having these things add to your life?"

"I am free of worry, my bills are paid on time, and I have more time to enjoy life."

"How do you *feel* when you have these things?"

"I feel happy and peaceful."

So the essence of the goal of wanting a new job is ultimately to feel happy and peaceful. Once we can define the energetic essence, and through visualization or imagination, *feel* ourselves having the experience of achieving our goal, it is then possible for it to manifest.

It is also important, as the Lemurians are reminding us, to *know* that your prayer is answered, and it is taking the highest possible form. So when we pray we are not asking or begging for something to happen; we are confidently giving thanks that it is *done!* And so it *is*!

Sample Prayers of Intention for a Healing Session

Creator, Infinite Spirit, Mother Father Divine:

We are here before you as instruments of peace and healing and we offer ourselves as servants of the light.

We call upon only the highest and most sacred spiritual energies to be with us, to guide us, to share love, healing and wisdom with us; we send them our love; and we welcome them.

We raise ourselves up to receive healing for our highest good and the highest good of all concerned.

We offer ourselves as clear and open channels for the highest forms of the healing rays to flow through.

We give thanks that our personalities, egos and expectations stand aside, so the healing energies will flow in their clearest and truest form.

Creator we give thanks for the blessings of this healing and we know that through your love, it is done.

And So It Is

That is a very powerful prayer to begin a healing session with, but let's not forget the simple prayer.

Dear God:

Thank you for helping me heal.

Thank you that I am happy, prosperous and peaceful.

Thank you for my many blessings.

Thank you that I am the essence of Universal Love and Compassion.

And So It Is.

Symbols in Healing

Symbols have been used for centuries to represent different elements of spirituality. The symbols used in Karuna Reiki' are transcendental in nature, meaning they are connected directly to the God consciousness. Each symbol is a representation of a unique vibration and serves as a key to activate certain frequencies of energy. There are many ways to activate the energies of the symbols. They can be drawn in the air or over the hands or body. They can be visualized, projected from the eyes, or the brow chakra or their names can be chanted silently or aloud.

As we become experienced with these frequencies we often come to a point where we can activate the symbols by simply thinking of them and stating a sacred intention during a prayer. It is not the symbol itself that holds healing power, but the combination of the attunement to the symbols, our sacred intention, prayer, and the willingness to heal that unlocks the symbols' healing power.

The Karuna Reiki system includes some symbols that are used in other systems of healing. However, through the process of the attunement, the Karuna symbols and the nature of the Karuna energy itself, carry their own distinct vibration. Therefore, they function differently than similar symbols do when they are used to activate other energies.

Attunement to Karuna Reiki and the Symbols

Attunement can be defined as the act of "matching vibration" with a specific spiritual energy or frequency of light. Attunements raise the vibration of an individual. They can take place through initiation from one person to another, through spiritual or energetic practice, or in rare instances through spontaneous occurrence.

The ability to channel Karuna Reiki is passed on from a person who has been attuned as a Karuna Reiki Master and trained in the attunement technique, to a person wishing to receive an initiation attunement.

One of the things that takes place in a Karuna Reiki attunement is that our subtle energy system, or etheric bodies, clear and release denser energies and they are strengthened so that we are capable of holding higher frequencies of light for longer periods of time. This is necessary because Karuna Reiki contains intense frequencies that were not available to the earth until the 1990s.

With the rapid acceptance of Karuna Reiki energy by healers around the world, we find that the strength of the Karuna energy is increasing exponentially as more people are attuned, or receiving Karuna treatments. As the strength of Karuna Reiki ascends, the power of the attunement to clear and fortify our subtle bodies is intensified as well.

Learning Karuna Reiki

Karuna Reiki is taught only by Registered Karuna Reiki Masters. These teachers have agreed to abide by a code of ethics, minimum teaching standards, a standard curriculum, and to do the attunements as they were developed by the International Center for Reiki Training (ICRT).

All attunements must be given in person rather than at a distance or over the internet. All Registered Karuna Reiki Masters have a lineage which can be traced to a teacher licensed by the International Center for Reiki Training, and ultimately to William Rand. Please refer to the section on the registration process later in this book.

Karuna Reiki is most often taught to individuals who are experienced Usui Reiki Masters, however it is possible to learn Karuna Reiki as a practitioner.

There are actually four levels of the energy:

Karuna Reiki I - Practitioner Level

This level is taught to people who are Usui Reiki Advanced Practitioners. To learn the practitioner levels of Karuna Reiki, the student must have previously been attuned to the second level Usui symbols, as well as the traditional Usui Master symbol, at the practitioner level. Some schools call this pre-requisite Advanced Reiki, or 3a.

Four symbols are taught in this level, and an attunement to those symbols at the practitioner frequency is given.

Karuna Reiki II - Practitioner Level

The pre-requisite for this level is Karuna Reiki Practitioner Level I. Four additional symbols are taught in this level, and the attunement to these symbols is given.

Karuna Reiki I - Master Level

This level is taught to people who are experienced Usui Reiki Masters. This level includes attunement to the same four symbols taught in Karuna Reiki Practitioner I, plus three Karuna Reiki Master symbols.

Karuna Reiki II - Master Level

The pre-requisite for this level is Karuna Reiki Master Level I. This level includes attunement to the same four symbols taught in Karuna Reiki Practioner II, plus the three Karuna Reiki Master symbols, which increase the power of the practitioner symbols.

If one wants to become a Karuna Reiki Master and they are already an experienced Usui Reiki Master, it is not necessary to first become a Karuna I & II practitioner. Masters are trained in a three-day intensive workshop, or special 4-7 day intensive retreats. They move through all the practitioner and master levels of the energy during these programs.

Although not necessary, it is possible to first become a Karuna Reiki I & II practitioner, and later take the master training. This is a matter of personal preference and choice.

One of the most common questions asked by students regarding Reiki training in general is "When am I ready to move on to the next level?" Some schools have strict rules about this that are measured in months or years. I don't find this chronological measurement to be as effective as the student's inner knowing and the wisdom of the Reiki energy.

Some students may practice Reiki many times a day and they are ready to advance in their training sooner than someone who practices once a week or once a month. I will emphasize many times in this book that experience with the energy is the best teacher. Once a student has so much experience with their current level and the techniques they learned that their heart is asking for more . . . they are ready.

Always remember to listen to the wisdom of your heart.

Uses for Karuna Reiki Symbols

In defining the uses of the symbols here, I will be introducing you to the names that represent the Karuna symbols. I will not be including drawings of the symbols as I feel that doing so serves no constructive purpose. As mentioned earlier the symbols themselves have no power without an attunement. They are also most effective when one is thoroughly trained in a Karuna Reiki class.

The Usui Reiki tradition asks practitioners not to reveal the names or the form of the Usui symbols to one who is not attuned to them. I have honored that tradition for many years and continue to do so.

Therefore, the decision to print the names of the Karuna symbols was not an easy one. The Karuna symbols are deeply sacred to me, and I did not want to compromise their sacred nature in anyway. I talked it over with William Rand and several other Karuna Masters and we agreed that it would be easier for the reader to understand what symbol is being referred to if we used the name for the symbol rather than a coded reference to it. As long as the reader understands that the name has no power without the attunement that comes in a Karuna Reiki class, then no harm would be done.

We also decided not to print the actual symbols because we feel that this helps preserve their sacred nature, and maintains the spiritual integrity of the Karuna Reiki system.

The use of the symbol names will help clearly communicate the techniques included in this book. I hope this helps Karuna practitioners more clearly understand how the symbols can be used to assist with personal problems and world situations. I also hope that this knowledge will encourage a more frequent use of Karuna Reiki, which will in turn bring more of this advanced healing energy to the planet and assist in our evolution.

Out of respect for the Usui Reiki tradition, I do not include the names or form of the Usui symbols in this book. I recognize that other authors have published the symbols, but I have chosen personally not to reveal their names or their form to anyone who has not received the sacred attunement to the Usui symbols and the specific training in their use.

When I mention the Usui symbols, I will reference them by their functions; the power symbol, the mental/emotional symbol, the distant healing symbol, the Usui master symbol, the Tibetan master symbol, and the Tibetan chakra-balancing symbol.

Students learn how to draw and activate the Karuna symbols when they participate in a Karuna Reiki class.

The names and a summary of basic use of the symbols are:

Karuna Reiki Level I

Zonar — Past life issues, child abuse, cellular healing, spiritual anesthetic, preparation

Halu — Unconscious patterns, shadow self, abuse issues, psychological or psychic "attack"

Harth — Relationships, addictive behavior, develop healthy habits, develop Universal Compassion

Rama — Harmonizes chakras, focus, lower chakras, goals, manifestation, grounding, sealing session, clearing objects, rooms and property.

Karuna Reiki Level II

Gnosa — Align with higher self, learning, communication, creativity, motor skills

Kriya — Grounding, manifestation, priorities, healing humanity,

Iava — Personal Divine power, co-dependence, reality awareness, empower goals, heal the Earth

Shanti — Create peace, trust in life, insomnia, fear, panic, clairvoyance

Karuna Reiki Level 1 Symbols

The level one symbols can each be used alone, or they can be used in sequence for a complete healing session.

Zonar

One of the first things that I learned from using Zonar is that it has the ability to act as a spiritual anesthetic. By this I mean it has the ability to prepare the recipient to allow Karuna Reiki energy to penetrate their subtle and physical bodies deeply while minimizing or eliminating potential physical, mental or emotional discomfort. Because of this I tend to use this symbol at the beginning of all treatments.

Zonar helps us heal from deep within the very atoms and cells of our beings. Our bodies carry memories of all our experiences in this life and other lifetimes. Zonar helps us heal on the cellular level. There is more information about cellular healing in the Karuna Reiki and Cellular Healing section of this book.

Zonar primarily focuses on preparation for cellular release, and therefore helps prepare us for healing of issues relating to past lives and abuse issues, or trauma from our current lifetime.

Keywords: Preparation, anesthetic, cellular healing, abuse, past lives

Crystals/Stones that can enhance the qualities of Zonar: Alexandrite placed on the heart center, Elestial Quartz placed on the third eye.

Halu

Halu is a level I symbol that expands upon the qualities of Zonar. Once the recipient of a treatment is prepared to process deep healing through the application of Zonar, they are ready to receive the healing power of Halu.

Halu is a penetrating energy that moves into the various levels of our subtle energy field, our physical being, and flows through levels of our conscious and unconscious mind. Halu finds areas where we are holding unhealthy patterns and sends a strong, laser-like beam of light into these areas. When I have been fortunate enough to clairvoyantly observe this, what I have seen has been an area where the emotional and mental bodies meet. Energy has gathered between these bodies that is composed of compressed geometric shapes and look something like a chain or wires that are tangled together. When Halu's "laser light" streams into the area, the snarled energy becomes less dense and the tangles appear to relax and unravel. As this happens new energy patterns begin to form from the energy that is clearing and realigning.

Halu also helps us identify and embrace our sub-personalities, or shadow selves. These are aspects of who we are, that for one reason or another we have chosen to deny, hide or ignore. Perhaps we have addictive behavior qualities that we pretend are not there. Maybe we have done things that we feel guilty about. We may have been conditioned to be-lieve that our special talents and abilities are detriments rather than gifts. For example, those who have highly developed psychic senses, or children who have been diagnosed ADD or hyperactive simply because the "main-stream" systems do not understand them.

If guilt is what we are dealing with we have the opportunity to learn to accept what we have done, recognize that we did the best we were capable of doing at the time, and we have grown because of the experi-ence. If denial of our uniqueness is the issue, we learn compassion and acceptance for ourselves through the use of Halu.

When we deny a part of who we are, we are not allowing ourselves to acknowledge the value that all of our experiences have in forming who we are in the moment. We know that Universal Compassion is the true es-sence of Karuna Reiki, and we have learned that Halu helps us share compassion with all aspects of our being; even those which we have felt are unacceptable.

Healing our sub-personalities can help us end self-sabotaging behavior and fears of succeeding, or living a joyous, prosperous, peaceful, loving life.

Halu goes a step beyond Zonar in the healing of abuse and past life issues. Where Zonar helps to anesthetize us, Halu identifies where the energy is held and helps to release it. In the same way that Halu helps to heal these issues, it also helps us identify instances of psychic or psychological attack that we create or attract while our higher self is helping us create circumstances from which we can learn and heal.

Keywords: Self-acceptance, abuse issues, psychic/psychological attack, sub-personalities, shadow self.

Crystals/Stones that can enhance the qualities of Halu: Green Obsidian worn near the heart or solar plexus, Picture Jasper, Hematite, Rhodocrosite.

Harth

If the Karuna Reiki system had only one symbol, I feel it would be Harth. The symbol Harth represents the energetic essence of Universal compassion. I experience Harth as the key to the Karuna Reiki energy.

Nearly every person who is attracted to healing work is a compassionate person. We are often very empathetic, actually feeling the pain or emotional trauma of people, animals, or elements of nature. We think of having compassion as a positive trait. However, is it helpful to be compassionate and feel dis-empowered?

Have you ever watched the news to see a tragic story and felt totally helpless? You may feel total compassion, yet you do nothing. Taking action on our compassionate feelings is the key, and this is what Harth can do for us. Harth inspires us and guides us to right action while helping us understand that practicing compassionate action brings more joy to the earth plane and is a wonderful blessing.

Harth teaches the important lesson that we must first experience compassion for ourselves before we can truly feel compassion for any other being. It is relatively easy to feel what I consider to be "surface compassion" for others. This is very different than Universal Compassion that we defined earlier. Universal compassion knows no boundaries and sees all of creation as one. Therefore it is not possible to truly hold the essence of Universal Compassion for someone and not for our self or for all beings.

I once heard of a person who said she could not use Harth, that it caused her to feel very uncomfortable or even frightened. Knowing only a little of her personality and circumstances I was still able to understand why this might be. She openly expresses mistrust for men as a result of abusive experiences in her life. In order for her to accept Universal Compassion she would need to open her heart more than she was ready to do at the time. She was using self-imposed boundaries to feel safe.

Through my years of experience with Reiki I have found that whenever a person feels a particular repulsion to any symbol that is normally the one they most need to use for the next phase of their healing.

The walls we place to protect us from focusing on the areas we need to heal are like comfort zones. Karuna Reiki helps us to quickly dissolve those walls, and move out of those comfort zones so we can grow stronger. It also helps us make these changes while we are embraced by Divine Love.

So if we will simply recognize when those walls are present, we have the opportunity to find the courage to use our healing tools so we can grow and move forward to the next step on our life path.

Once we begin to understand and integrate the vibration of Universal Compassion, many other aspects of our lives begin to align. We experience changes in our relationships, our habits, and our ability to contact the spiritual Masters.

When we begin to view life through the eyes of God, we find ourselves being more tolerant in relationships, or perhaps we finally find the courage to set clear boundaries. It may seem strange to think of boundaries when Harth helps us acknowledge our oneness with all there is, but as we move through life we sometimes encounter relationships that must end in order for both parties to grow. These are the boundaries I am speaking of.

When using Harth to heal relationship issues, it is important to identify the life force that the relationship itself has. For example, if I am having difficulty communicating with a friend, the problem isn't really my friend and it isn't me either. The problem is where our energies blend and create a unique life form. I find it helpful to select a crystal or other object that represents the relationship. I then invoke the Usui distant symbol, the mental and emotional symbol, and Harth together while I send Reiki and Karuna Reiki to the relationship through the object.

The most common result of this type of energy transmission is that both my friend and I will see one another's point of view more clearly and develop a deeper understanding of one another.

When Harth is used in treatment it calls the full power of the Karuna Reiki energy into the session and can help heal issues of the heart, both physically and emotionally.

Because Harth helps us have compassion for ourselves, it inspires and energizes us to develop healthy habits. For example if you would like to eat a healthier diet or exercise on a regular basis, meditating with Harth or chanting its name while you cook or workout can help healthy habits form.

Because addictive behaviors hold the opposite energy of a healthy habit, Harth is also helpful in healing addictions. It raises the love and compassion vibration so much that it becomes very difficult to do things that are harmful to us.

A wonderful benefit of living in a state of Universal compassion is that we are then better able to communicate with spiritual beings and masters who hold this vibration for the earth like Mother Mary, Kuan Yin, Avalokiteshavara, Jesus and Lady Master Nada. These and other great beings of light are available to assist our planet in its evolution. Raising our vibration so that we can communicate more clearly with spiritual masters helps to accelerate our awareness of the co-creative power we have to simply awaken to the age of peace and healing.

Keywords: compassion, action, spiritual communication, unity, issues of the heart, relationships, healthy habits, healing addictive behaviors, calls in the full power of Karuna Reiki

Crystals/Stones that can enhance the qualities of Harth: White calcite, green smithsonite, and spectrolite.

Rama

The final symbol in Level I Karuna Reiki is Rama.

One of the most powerful things that Rama does is harmonize our upper and lower chakras, which allows our upper chakras to attract Divine inspiration into our mental body. It then moves through our emotional body and ultimately through our entire chakra system so that we can bring this inspiration into form on the manifest plane through our lower chakras.

Before doing this though, Rama helps to heal the lower chakras so that we can be grounded and focused. The use of Rama facilitates us in calling all our energy back into our bodies. Many of us have learned "survival techniques" due to trauma, abuse, or fear. One of the most common is the tendency to partially leave our physical bodies when we experience something that feels uncomfortable or too painfully familiar. This leaves our energy scattered and our physical being incomplete or separate from the wholeness that we are striving to achieve. Symptoms of this might be feeling spacey, unfocused, listless, disorganized, and unable to complete tasks, etc.

In shamanic healing, soul retrieval is a powerful technique of calling back fragmented parts of the soul. These parts are believed to have separated from the core soul essence of a person due to trauma. I have found that using Usui and Karuna Reiki, including Rama provides the same result as a shamanic soul retrieval. However, I feel that the process is gentler when using the various forms of Reiki energy.

When people require this work, they are often very fragile. I do not recommend attempting Karuna Reiki soul retrieval on others until you have worked with it for yourself. It is best to have extensive experience giving Reiki and Karuna Reiki treatments to others before attempting soul retrieval work. I don't say this because there is anything to fear from doing this because we know that Reiki never causes harm. I do say this because the more experience you have with the energies and working with others, the more adept you will be at intuiting precisely which energies to call in to facilitate this type of healing.

Rama is also very helpful in treatment to clear dense blockages in the etheric field and to close a session and bring the recipient fully back into their body.

When you need to make a sudden adjustment to a vibrational change, such as when you are traveling, using Rama can help you adjust to the new vibration when you arrive at your destination.

I learned this very well through multiple personal experiences, but one in particular still makes me smile. I traveled to Glastonbury, England to teach Karuna Reiki with William Rand at Stonehenge. My schedule was very full at the time and I only had one day after my flight from the U.S. to adjust to the time difference and the vibration of Glastonbury before I was scheduled to teach. William, a dear friend, teacher and a seasoned visitor to Glastonbury, was excited to show me the sites. So immediately upon my arrival I dropped my suitcases off in my room and we were off to tour.

One of the first things we did was hike the Tor. It is not particularly high, nor did it appear to be a very strenuous endeavor. After all, I had hiked Mt. Kurama for 2 solid days, 7 hours each day, and done attunements on top of Bell Rock in Sedona several times. So the Tor actually looked like a stroll in the park. Much to my dismay, I realized about 15 minutes into the hike that I was out of breath, my legs ached, and I could barely go on. Being a bit stubborn, I forced myself to continue, but my need to stop and catch my breath grew more and more frequent. I finally explained to William what was happening to me. He reminded me that I had just made a very rapid change in vibration as a result of the long flight and being in the energy of Glastonbury and suggested that I use Rama. I felt my ego creeping in a bit because I was embarrassed that I hadn't thought of this myself, after all I teach that in all my classes.

Immediately I invoked Rama, called the energy through my entire body and envisioned the symbol on the bottom of both my feet. I waited a few minutes and I could feel my body adjusting, almost as if my actual atoms and cells were realigning. When the sensations stopped, I was then able to continue the hike and the rest of our touring with no discomfort.

I also use Rama to strengthen the light in any situation, particularly when I enter a room that seems to have stagnant or dense energy. Rama helps to lift out anything of a lower frequency and replace it with radiant light.

Keywords: harmonizes chakras, focus, clarity, soul retrieval, manifestation, Divine alignment, grounding, closing session, space clearing and recharging

Crystals/Stones that can enhance the qualities of Rama: Amethyst, blue calcite, garnet, star garnet, ametrine.

The Karuna I symbols in general can assist the practitioner in healing specific conditions as well as connecting with specific guides, angels and masters. This is explored during Karuna Reiki classes.

Using the Karuna I Symbols in Treatment

As you have read, each of the level I symbols have very specific purposes. I recommend to my students that they meditate with each of the symbols daily for one week initially, and then after they have meditated for the first four weeks, that they choose a symbol they feel is particularly powerful for them and work with it for 21 days. This is to help them develop a deeper understanding of the symbols and to enhance their personal healing.

Now that you understand that each symbol can be used alone, let me summarize why they also work well together, particularly when used in the sequence in which they have been presented; 1-Zonar 2-Halu 3-Harth 4-Rama

The first part of a treatment is space preparation, which I address thoroughly in the section on creating sacred space.

Next I say a prayer of intention in which:

1. I give thanks that I am a clear and open channel for only the highest forms of the healing rays to flow through.

2. I give thanks that only the highest and most sacred spiritual energies are present to guide me and that I am completely open to their guidance, wisdom and inspiration.

3. I give thanks that my personality and ego stand aside so that the energy will flow in its clearest and truest form.

4. I give thanks that the healing serves the highest good of all concerned, and state the specific focus for the session.

5. Finally I give thanks in advance for this healing acknowledging that through Divine Love, it is done.

I open a session with Zonar to prepare the client. Remember Zonar is the spiritual anesthetic that prepares us on a cellular level for deep healing.

Next I use Halu to find the areas that are in need of healing, and to disperse the dense energies with a laser-like beam of light.

The third symbol, Harth, then fills the space that has been cleared with the full power of Karuna Reiki, Universal Compassion in action.

Rama is used to call all the client's energy back into their body, and to help seal the healing energies in so the healing will last for an extended period of time.

So you see, even though the symbols are powerful when used individually, there is a specific treatment flow that can be achieved when they are used in sequence.

I would also like to explain that Usui Reiki works very well with Karuna energy, and that I almost always weave the two together.

There are no particular hand positions that are unique to Karuna. I find it works best for me to begin a treatment by calling in all the Usui, Tibetan and Karuna Reiki symbols. I then use the Reiji-ho and Byosen scanning methods of asking the energy to guide my hands to where energy is first needed. When I find the first area to work, I then invoke Zonar and treat the area until the energy stops flowing. At this point I repeat the scan asking if any other area of the body needs Zonar. If my hands are drawn to another area, I treat that part of the person. I continue until I have no more indications that Zonar is needed.

Next I call in Halu and repeat the process above using Halu. I do the same thing for each of the four symbols. If at anytime I am inspired or intuitively guided to bring in an Usui symbol, or a different Karuna symbol I always follow that guidance. I then go back to the standard sequence.

Karuna Reiki° Level II Symbols

The level two symbols also can each be used alone, or they can be woven in between the Level I symbols as your intuition guides you.

Although I have great respect and gratitude for the Karuna I symbols, it wasn't until my attunement to the Karuna II symbols that I fully realized all healing symbols are living beings! My awareness was heightened so much that I could see, hear and feel the life force pulsing and flowing through and from the symbols.

An exercise that continues to help me develop this ability is to imagine the symbol cocooned in a glowing, radiant ball of light floating at my soul star chakra (6-8 inches above the crown of my head). I breathe in through my crown, drawing the ball of light containing the symbol into my head and down to my heart. Placing my awareness at my heart center and focusing on my breathing, I feel the light that the symbol contains growing brighter and the energy growing stronger. When my heart feels like it is glowing, I exhale with all my power and allow the energy to flow through my entire body. When my whole body feels as if it is glowing I bring my awareness back to my heart center and send a beam of light, containing an image of the symbol out in front of me, almost as a movie projector sends photographic impressions onto a screen.

I sit in meditation with the energy filling my entire being, and the symbol's image floating out in front of me. I experience the symbol with my inner vision, watching, listening and feeling everything it wants to communicate with me.

Sometimes the symbols pulsate, twirl, dance, speak, breathe, or even change form.

As you experience the vastness of Karuna Reiki I recommend this technique to deepen your understanding of its limitless nature.

Gnosa

Gnosa - means knowledge or wisdom. Remember that Karuna can be defined as compassionate action accompanied by wisdom.

Gnosa assists us in connecting with the Divine Mind through our higher self. The Divine Mind contains the infinite wisdom that guides the unfolding of the evolutionary plan for each of us as individuals, for humanity as a collective and for the earth.

When we connect with this infinite wisdom at the level of our higher self, it can be challenging to bring that knowledge into the physical plane. When we work with the energy of Gnosa, this becomes much easier. Essentially, Gnosa helps us access wisdom through our higher self and anchor it into our physical bodies. This helps us to BE our higher self in our daily activities.

Imagine . . . your higher self is fully present in your body right now. You have direct access to the Divine Mind to learn anything you want to learn. You can effortlessly grasp concepts that once were difficult to understand. You can energetically integrate them into your mental body, anchoring them with Gnosa. Once this knowledge is present in your mental body, you can call upon it at any time. Although at this moment you are simply imagining these things, it is possible for them to become a reality with continued use of the energy transmitted through Gnosa.

We also experience enhanced communication abilities when we use Gnosa to help heal. In interpersonal communications it becomes easier to understand what someone else is trying to say. Our higher self is able to remove emotional or mental blockages to clear communication. When we are communicating as our higher self we help others raise their vibration and communicate more clearly as well.

Gnosa also has a direct effect on the nervous system making it easier to develop skills that require motor coordination such as dancing, athletics, or playing musical instruments.

During a retreat on the Big Island of Hawaii in 1999, I was presented with an opportunity to learn middle-eastern drumming. Although many people who have attended my classes or heard me speak in public might find it hard to believe, I am actually a bit of an introvert and quite shy. Learning something new in the presence of other people tends to make me a little nervous.

I listened intently to Michael, our teacher, as he demonstrated perfectly a variety of middle-eastern rhythms. I would try to mimic what I had just heard him play, but my hands would not do what my mind was asking them to.

So I struggled along feeling more and more insecure and intimidated by my apparent lack of musical talent. Suddenly I remembered Gnosa. So I paused, called Gnosa in with a breath through the crown of my head, into my heart, and let the energy flow down my arms and out my hands into the drum. I channeled Gnosa into the drum for a few minutes. As I was doing this I began to feel more at ease. When I felt as if the energy had shifted from a strong surge to a steady flow, I again attempted to mimic the rhythms Michael was sharing with us. I was amazed at how much easier it was and how natural it felt. Interestingly, I began to feel as if the rhythms were very familiar to me, as if memories of another time were streaming into my consciousness.

Artists, musicians, writers and other creative types often find that Gnosa helps dissolve blocks to the creative process. I know an artist who is beginning to relate to color in an entirely new way since her Karuna Reiki training. In meditation, many of us have experienced colors that just don't seem to exist in this dimension. These colors are somehow more vibrant and full of light, and they do exist on the inner planes. The use of Gnosa to connect with the Divine Mind has the potential of teaching us how to reprogram what we currently understand about color and to bring these higher color vibrations into form on the manifest plane. I am beginning to see glimpses of this in my artist friend's paintings.

When I sit down to write I always invoke Gnosa. First I sit in silence for a few moments, I then focus on my breathing. When I have connected with Gnosa, I simply ask to be taken into the theta state of consciousness and to connect with the light of the Divine Mind.

When I feel this connection, I envision a column of pearlescent white light streaming from this infinite intelligence, into the light of my soul group, into the light of my soul, and into my physical being.

I inhale this light very deeply and feel it almost sparkling in the very cells of my body. My breathing gradually brings me more into a creative state of consciousness, and then I simply begin to write. This process makes writing almost effortless.

I have also found that combining Gnosa with the Usui mental and emotional symbol can be helpful for people dealing with attention deficit disorder. Frenetic mental patterns are realigned and it becomes easier to focus.

Keywords: Wisdom, knowledge, creative process, communication, Divine Mind, motor skills.

Crystals/Stones that can enhance the qualities of Gnosa: Alabaster, yellow sapphire, emerald, zoisite.

Kriya

Kriya means action in Sanskrit.

Kriya helps us put our goals, dreams and visions into action. Kriya is unique in the manner that it flows, or perhaps I should say how it does *not* flow. Normally when I work with healing energies I sense the normal sensations of energy moving, such as temperature changes, pulsing, tingling, electrical impulses, etc. In addition, I often feel like the energy is flowing through me like liquid light.

Kriya is unique in that the energy is more like a constant vibration, a wave pouring forth from a sea of light: a wave that is always moving forward. When I channel Kriya I feel as if I AM this wave.

The most common use for Kriya is grounding by actually moving life force energy from the crown chakra, down through the entire energy system and into the earth.

Kriya can also be used to do a form of the technique know as a chakra connection. The symbol is placed at the crown chakra, and then light flows down to the brow chakra. Kriya is then placed in the brow chakra, it heals the brow and the light flows down to the throat chakra, and so on. At each chakra Kriya clears blockages and opens the center to more light until the chakra ultimately overflows with light. This excess light then streams down into the next chakra.

Because Kriya has a tendency to move energy down through the chakra system from the upper energy centers to the lower, it is an energy key that can be used for manifesting goals. It is particularly powerful when used in conjunction with positive affirmation, Gnosa, and the Usui mental and emotional symbol. Gnosa helps to form goals from the wisdom of the higher mind, the mental and emotional symbol helps to anchor the affirmation into the etheric field, and Kriya brings the essence of the goal into the physical body helping to anchor the goal in the form of light into our cells. When this process is complete, we are better equipped to put our plans and goals into action.

The process mentioned above can also be used to prioritize your goals. There was a time in the not too distant past that I was a to-do-list-aholic. I would make a list of perhaps 20 things that I felt MUST be done on that day. I would work very hard to accomplish them all, and if I didn't succeed, at times I felt guilty or disappointed in myself. Over a period of time I started to notice that, because the situations in life are constantly changing, something that was at the top of my to do list a month ago, that I did accomplish, no longer matters because circumstances changed. Consequently I put a lot of time and energy into something that makes no contribution to myself or anyone else. What a waste of energy!

So I began to wonder what would happen if I let the higher mind set my priorities, and if Karuna Reiki could help. I discovered that by using Gnosa, Kriya and the Usui mental and emotional symbol I could prioritize my goals in a much more effective way.

This process works because we are connecting with the Divine mind first and touching into our goals as pure energy. When viewing our goals as energy it is easy for our higher self to ascertain which goals contain the most light in a given moment.

To do this, simply connect with the infinite intelligence holding the intention that you are going to manifest the tasks, which will produce the greatest positive impact on your life or the lives of others in this very moment. You can use the symbols as described above.

Now, this does not mean that you are going to focus only on profound things. Sometimes taking out the garbage is the most important task in the moment and at other times sending healing energy to a war torn area of the world is most important. Let your connection to infinite wisdom with the help of Kriya establish your priorities and you may find that your life flows much more smoothly.

Keywords: Grounding, manifestation, priorities, chakra clearing and alignment.

Crystals/Stones that can enhance the qualities of Kriya: Fire agate, golden topaz, red jasper, yellow smithsonite, spectrolite, blue tiger's eye.

Iava

Iava - is a symbol that relates directly to our personal Divine Power. When I first started doing Karuna Reiki treatments for others I realized that I was guided to use Iava on nearly every client.

It is inherent within Iava to keep our energy clear from thought forms projected by others, or even from our own fears. Many people create their life according to what other people expect them to do, or what they think they should do to conform to society. Living like this is energetically draining and blocks us from claiming our own power. We prevent ourselves from listening to and following our heart.

That statement, "Listen to your heart" is used so often, that sometimes it sounds a bit cliché. However, it takes on greater meaning with the understanding that our soul communicates directly with our heart, or more specifically our heart triad, or heart trinity. The heart triad is a special etheric link between our heart, sacred heart, and ascending heart chakras with the wisdom of our soul. The collective energy formed by the heart trinity is also known as the etheric heart.

Because of this special communication link we have with our soul, our heart centers are always aligned with Divine will and constantly trying to guide us.

Iava can help to keep the etheric heart clear of influences that might otherwise distract us or cause us to be afraid of creating the life we were born to live.

Many of us are actually afraid of that word … Power. In today's world it has so many negative connotations. However, whenever I speak of power in this book, I am speaking of Divine Love. The only true power is Love.

Marianne Williamson once wrote about our "greatest fear".

Our Greatest Fear

"Our greatest fear is not that we are inadequate.
Our greatest fear is that we are powerful beyond measure.
It is our light, not our darkness that most frightens us.
We ask ourselves, "Who am I to be brilliant, talented, fabulous?"
Actually, who are you not to be? You are a child of God.
Your playing small doesn't serve the world.
There's nothing enlightened about shrinking so that
other people won't feel insecure around you.
We were born to make manifest the glory of God that is within us.
It's not just in some of us, it's in ALL of us.
As we let our own light shine, we unconsciously give
other people permission to do the same.
As we are liberated from our own fear,
our presence automatically liberates others."

These words speak directly to my soul. I know that what she says here is true for many. We have a soul knowing that we ARE the power of God's love incarnate, and we are absolutely limitless. However, it often feels so much more comfortable to "play small". By stepping into our true power and embracing it we instantly are in complete alignment with our Divine purpose. Iava is a magnificent healing tool to help us achieve this goal.

The healing qualities of Iava can be particularly helpful in resolving co-dependent issues in relationships. Since Iava helps us create our own reality, it also helps us release the sense of being responsible for other people.

I was taught that Iava is also a powerful symbol for earth healing, and I have found this to be true in the sense that it helps us harmonize our consciousness with all aspects of the nature kingdom.

Becoming the Solstice Moon

I have had many experiences using Iava to connect with elements of nature. One such experience happened when I was teaching in Australia. It was the winter solstice there and the moon was full. I was looking out the window admiring the brilliance of the moon when I felt guided to invoke the Usui distant symbol and Iava with the intention of connecting with the consciousness of the moon. No sooner had I done this than I felt my spirit lift from my body and I experienced an incredible, joyous journey. First I felt like I WAS the moon. As soon as I realized that...I became the moonlight, and then the moonlight shimmering within a cloud, and then the cloud, and so on. During this journey I experienced being a raindrop, the ocean, a tree, the wind, a grain of sand, etc. It was a profound experience for me.

Karuna Reiki and the Healing Tree

A few years after my experience in Australia I had decided to move from my home of 20 years. I put all of my belongings in storage and ventured to a place in Colorado that my heart was calling me to. During the move I lifted some things and hurt my back. I then immediately hopped into the jeep for 20 hours to drive to Colorado. Riding in a car that long with an injured back is not something I would recommend.

When I arrived in Colorado I was in excruciating pain. I was traveling with my friends, Michael and Max as we explored the San Isabel National Forest. Michael is an intuitive and very gifted healer. I was in so much pain I barely realized that he had suddenly stopped the jeep by the side of the road and was nearly pulling me out of it. He said "Come on, I have a good feeling about this place". So I hobbled behind him to a place in the forest. I was almost magnetized to a place between the trees where sun was streaming down onto the red earth. The area had a very gentle curving slope. I lay down on the earth to allow the arch of my back to merge with the curve of the earth. The ground was so warm and the sunlight felt wonderful. Michael began to give me a Reiki treatment as I asked the earth to help me heal and invoked lava.

Moments later I heard a "voice" from behind us say; "I can help you". I looked around and there was no one there. I asked Michael if he had heard anything and he said "No". So I went back to my conscious connection with the earth beneath me. I heard it again! "I can help you".

I sat up slowly and looked in the direction of the "voice" and noticed one particular pine tree that appeared to be glowing. I walked over to it and instinctively turned to place my back against it. My feet settled down into the roots, with one foot slightly higher than the other. I then reached up above my head and there were two broken branches. I grasped them with my hands, and they were at different levels. I realized that my body was being encouraged to stretch into an unusual position. So, with my arms raised above my head, grasping branches, and my feet nestled in the roots of the tree, I slowly pressed my spine against the trunk of the tree. Instantly the vertebrae in my back realigned and the pain I had experienced for nearly a week was totally gone.

I was in awe. I told Michael what had happened and we were so thankful we both gave the tree a Reiki treatment.

I have also found that lava helps me live more consciously, and I have a keener awareness of the nature spirits.

Keywords: Personal power, Divine Will, co-dependence, earth healing, communicating with nature, nature spirits.

Crystals/Stones that can enhance the qualities of Iava: Aquamarine, red aventurine, charoite, and rutilated quartz.

Shanti

Shanti is Sanskrit for peace. The only thing that keeps us from being totally peaceful is fear. I feel the most powerful gift that Shanti brings to us is the ability to totally trust in the Divine and completely release our fears, our worries, our goals and our visions. When we let go in this way and trust that everything in life is part of the Divine Plan, we come to know that only that which is for our highest good will take place in our life, and being peaceful becomes a natural state of being.

Sometimes when we feel like things haven't gone well in our past, we grow to expect things to go wrong as a normal part of life. This type of mental pattern can be so energetically draining that it can create an inability to move forward in life, or even create illnesses such as chronic fatigue or fibromyalgia. Shanti is very effective in healing such mental patterning.

Shanti can help us begin to see all situations in our life as positive experiences because we have the opportunity to grow from our challenges, often even more than from our triumphs. When we begin to see situations that could be viewed as failures or tragedies as opportunities to grow, we find less in life to be fearful about.

I find that invoking Shanti through the following chant and then offering this prayer is very effective in helping me let go of worries and fears.

Om Shanti, Shanti, Om Shanti, Shanti Om Shanti, Shanti

Creator ... I give thanks for that which is for my highest good comes to me today; and only your love and light flow from me today ... And So It Is

Om Shanti, Shanti, Om Shanti, Shanti Om Shanti, Shanti

In Karuna classes, students learn other uses for Shanti including ways to increase clairvoyance and assist the healing of specific illnesses.

Keywords: Peace, trust, fear, clairvoyance.

Crystals/Stones that can enhance the qualities of Shanti: Volcanic ash, volcanic glass, kunzite, watermelon tourmaline, pink sapphire.

Using the Karuna Reiki°
Level II Symbols in Treatment

As I explained in the section on using the Karuna Reiki level I symbols that I ask my students to meditate with one symbol a week, and then after four weeks they select one symbol they are particularly drawn to. The practitioner then meditates with the selected symbol for 21 days. I suggest the same process with the level II symbols.

When using the level II symbols in treatment, they too can be used in sequence such as; Gnosa, Kriya, Iava and Shanti. However, the level II symbols are often woven in with the level I symbols. For example if a basic foundation for a treatment is Zonar, Halu, Harth and Rama, one might introduce level II symbols after Halu.

Let's consider the example of giving a treatment to a person who is experiencing creative blocks and would like to heal them. I might be guided to use:

· Zonar to prepare the person for deep healing

· Halu to locate and lift out energetic blocks related to the issue

· Gnosa to align the person's heart and mind with their higher self

· Iava to assist them in allowing their personal Divinity to flow into their work and to help them create reality in the highest form

· Rama and the Usui power symbol to anchor the energies into the body, manifest their work in the physical plane, and close and seal the session.

There is no absolute formula for blending the symbols together. It is most important for the practitioner to follow their intuition, but it is fine to weave the level I and II Karuna symbols together and also to include the Usui Reiki symbols.

Giving a Karuna Reiki Treatment

There are several steps in giving a treatment that I like to follow.

Preparing Sacred Space

A sacred space can be created anywhere, but it starts within our own heart, and flows from our oneness with the Divine essence of Mother Earth and the cosmos. Every sacred, or holy experience we have ever had becomes a part of who we are. We carry these experiences wherever we go, thus any place can be a sacred space.

I find it imperative to acknowledge, or create sacred space wherever I am. My entire home is treated as sacred space, not just one room, but the whole house the grounds and the region in which I live.

There are four very simple steps to creating sacred space:

1. Pray to give thanks for Divine assistance

2. Clear dense energies from the space

3. Infuse the space with the full power of Divine Love, Reiki, and Karuna Reiki energy

4. Pray to give thanks that the clearing and empowerment are complete and the energies are sealed in.

The first thing to do is to clear the energy in your "inner space" by balancing your chakras and calling in the Reiki energy, spiritual guides and the Masters. In doing this I begin with a prayer of sacred intention. Next I like to invoke all the Usui, Tibetan and Karuna Reiki symbols that I know.

I imagine the symbols one at a time forming as seeds of light in my heart center, growing brighter, and stronger, and larger until the light they are radiating flows out into and permeates my energy field. During this process I hold the intention that anything less than light is lifted from me, and it is replaced with the healing energies I am invoking.

After I have completed the self-preparation, I am ready to clear the physical space. I often burn sage or use an aromatherapy mist of sage oil, lemon oil, or sandalwood. This helps my physical senses recognize the cleansing process.

It may also be helpful to play music while you are clearing and charging the space. There are several pieces of music that I like to use specifically for space clearing. One is "Nomad" by Nomad, another is "Planet Drum" by Mickey Hart. I use them only for that purpose and that helps to hold the intention during a space clearing.

Next I use Rama, the Usui power symbol and Usui master symbol. I draw or beam them onto the four walls, the ceiling and floor. This clears any dense or darker energy from the room.

To fill the room with light, love and compassion I invoke all the Usui and Karuna Reiki symbols and beam them into the center of the room. I visualize the light that they contain permeating everything in the room and flowing outside the perimeter of the building and the grounds.

The final step is to give a prayer of thanks for the work that has been done, and for the healings that will take place in the sacred space that has been created.

The Healing Altar

Although not necessary, the creation of a healing altar in your space can add a personal touch that assists you, the practitioner, to focus and align with your source of spiritual sustenance and inspiration.

An altar can be set up on a special table, a shelf, or even a windowsill. Once you have identified the location for your altar, cleanse it by smudging, burning a white candle, using Reiki, and praying for the area to be cleared of any dense energy. Also pray that the area hold only the full light of Divine Love and Compassion.

The next step is to determine what objects you would like to place on your altar to empower it, and how you will place offerings on the altar. An offering may be a prayer request, or a photo of someone in need of healing, or a written intention of something that you would like to surrender and release to the Divine for healing or manifestation. You might place these offerings in a bowl or basket on the top of, or underneath your altar. There is no right way and no wrong way to place the offerings, listen to your heart.

Here are some ideas for objects you might like to place on your altar to empower it.

· Incense

· Candles

· Chimes or bells

· Prayer or meditation books

· Crystals

· Personal journal or diary

· Statues or photographs of spiritual beings

· Photographs of loved ones

· Feathers

· Seashells

· Wood

· Holy water

· Anointing oils

· Bowls, goblets or vessels

· Coins

· Sacred symbols

After you have selected the objects for your altar, I suggest that you pray and perform a blessing ceremony for the objects. You will want to use your intuition, and aesthetic sense to determine the correct placement on the altar for the sacred objects you have chosen.

It is important to allow ample time to set up your altar. Creating an altar can be a beautiful, personal sacred experience. An altar offers a focal point from which to commence any spiritual activity, or simply to begin your day from a point of center, balance and love.

Preparing the Client

The next step is to prepare the client. I begin by sending Reiki to the client using the Usui distant healing symbol prior to their arrival.

When the client arrives I sit with them and discuss what has brought them to the session. We talk about any physical, mental, or emotional reasons, which may have motivated them to come for a healing session.

Sometimes we find it appropriate to create a positive affirmation for them to hold in their thoughts as an intention for the session. I offer a prayer of intention on the client's behalf prior to starting the session and we align our higher selves to facilitate spiritual communication and discernment during the session. This allows the client's higher self and spiritual guides to communicate with my higher self and my guides regarding what the client needs.

There are many ways for a practitioner to align their higher self with the client's higher self. I use the Usui mental/emotional and Master symbols, and Gnosa. I invoke all three symbols and transmit the energy through my chakras and energy field, and then project that energy to the client with the intention that our higher selves are being aligned to facilitate communication and healing.

Often the next step would be for the client to be seated and meditate on their healing intention, while I channel a healing attunement* as preparation for a session on the treatment table. The healing attunement helps to lift away any energy that may be preventing the client from benefiting fully from the healing session.

When the healing attunement is complete I ask the client to lie down on the treatment table, and make sure they are comfortable. I check to see if they need a cushion or bolster under their knees to reduce strain on the lower back. I also ask if they want a pillow for their head, and if they prefer to be covered with a blanket. I find that when the client is very comfortable and warm it is easier for them to relax into the session and allow the healing to take place.

---

*Note: A healing attunement is a specific technique that is taught in many Usui/Tibetan Master classes. It is required in the curriculum of the International Center for Reiki Training

Channeling the Session

I begin the session with the strengthening of my light by drawing or visualizing the Usui Power symbol in my energy field and each of my chakras. I then invoke all the Karuna and Usui Reiki symbols.

I place my hands in prayer position at my heart and then bring them to my third eye as I invoke the Karuna and Usui energies and ask that my hands be guided to the areas of the body that need healing energy (this is the Japanese technique called Reiji-ho). I normally begin with Zonar and allow my hands to be placed on the body or in the etheric field as I am guided. This often feels like a magnetic pull to a specific position, or I sense a tingling or vibration in the area that I am to work. It may also be an inner knowing of where to place my hands.

I invoke additional symbols as I am guided, and when the energy seems to wane in a particular position, I again use Reiji-ho to discern the next hand placement and symbol to use.

I continue the session in this manner until it feels complete. This is normally results in a healing session that is 45 minutes to one hour in duration.

Closing the Session

I close the session with a prayer in which we give thanks for the healing that has taken place, the guidance we received and we acknowledge that healing will continue. I use Rama, and either the Usui Power symbol, or the Usui Master symbol to bring the client fully back into their body, and to seal the healing energies in and close the session.

House and Land Clearing

Throughout history the earth has seen great tragedies happen to humanity. Some have been caused by earth changes, some by war and violence. When the spirit leaves a physical body in the dying process, during sudden or violent conditions, it often attaches itself to another person, a structure or the earth itself.

Over the years I have been called to do several home and property clearings with Karuna Reiki.

Karuna works better for this than any other technique I have found. I feel this is because of the power of Universal Love and Universal compassion, and also the quality inherent in Karuna Reiki to release cellular memory from people and from the earth.

The following is a synopsis of an experience I had several years ago.

The House That Karuna Healed

We first walked through the doors of the House that Karuna healed in June of 1995. The 22 acres of rolling Kentucky countryside and forested areas upon which the house sits were breathtakingly beautiful. The sparkling stream flowing through the property has a special healing ambiance of its own. Though the land and the house were wonderful to look at, there was a certain heaviness or denseness in the energy when we first arrived.

From June through October we held healing sessions there and all levels of Reiki were taught. The house and the property were initiated to Reiki levels I and II, Advanced and Master, and ultimately Karuna Reiki via the many classes and practitioners that worked, learned and shared Reiki there.

The reason we had been drawn to this place to do our work was not apparent until the Karuna Reiki® class, which brought gifted Reiki Masters from all over the country to the House of Healing. Karuna is the energy of compassionate action and assists in strengthening one's connection with ascended, enlightened beings. It helps people heal at the cellular memory level. We were to learn it also heals the earth and discarnate spirits at this level as well.

During the class we became clairvoyantly aware (later historically verified) this land had been a battleground for centuries. Indian tribes fought over it for hunting ground, civil war battles were fought there, people who lived in this house died. We knew that there were many spirits attached to this anguished land, and the Reiki had made them receptive to healing and returning to the Source.

We were guided to a sensitive spot on the grounds, formed a circle, sent Karuna Reiki with specific channeled prayers to the land, and then we saw a magnificent physical manifestation. A column of iridescent white light appeared in the center of the circle, and what seemed like millions of flashing colored lights sped into it and they were transformed into white light. We had an inner knowing that these lights were the energetic mani-festation of those anguished spirits being healed by the Love of God through open channels of Karuna Reiki. The vibration of the property was instantly lighter, and the sense of peace that fell over the land cannot be described with words.

Our work is finished on the land where the House that Karuna healed stands, and today the Universe is guiding us to our next place of healing.

Blending Karuna and Usui Energies

You may have read elsewhere that students often claim Karuna Reiki is more powerful than Usui Reiki. I hesitate to compare any healing energy with another in that way. I always want to be cautious not to contribute to that all too prevalent sense among some people in the Reiki community that "My Reiki is better than your Reiki." I feel that Karuna and Usui energies are both equally powerful, but they express their power in different ways.

Each form of the Reiki energy has it unique characteristics, however they work extremely well together. I very often weave Usui energy between the Karuna frequencies in a treatment.

When I am working with a client who is new to energy work altogether, I am usually inclined to use primarily Usui energy in the first few treatments. I will however introduce one or two of the Karuna energies such as Iava, Rama, Harth or Shanti.

Since Karuna energy goes so deep, so quickly and has a tendency to lift us out of body, it is very nice to close a Karuna session with an Usui power or master symbol in addition to Rama. The Usui energy at the end of a very intense session is like a warm hug from the angels.

Once again, the most important thing for you to remember is to listen to your inner knowing when you are working with these energies. We pray in the beginning of our sessions for guidance; it is important that we trust the guidance when it comes, and also to express our gratitude for our prayer being answered.

Karuna Reiki Techniques

As we know, Reiki is spiritually guided life force energy. The integration of Karuna Reiki into a treatment has helped activate new channels for the guiding energies to communicate techniques that may be unique to a particular situation. The following are specific techniques that have been given to us over recent years that you may find helpful. Remember, however, always listen to the energy before working with any technique. Be sure using the technique feels right to you.

Addictive Behavior

This technique can help clear addictive behavior patterns and replace them with healthy patterns:

· Prayer of intention to release ego and activate all the Usui and Karuna Reiki energies, and to strengthen your light.

· Beam energy into the client's field with the intention of creating a healing link between the two of you.

· Activate Zonar, Harth and the Usui mental and emotional symbol, and the Usui master symbol. With one hand at the back of the head at the base of the skull and one hand over the brow chakra, transmit the energy until the flow stops. Move one hand over the solar plexus and one hand over the second chakra and continue to channel Zonar, Halu, Iava, Harth and the Usui mental and emotional symbol until the flow stops.

· Activate the Usui master symbol and Rama and channel these frequencies over the base chakra until the flow stops. Draw the Usui power symbol down the front of the body starting at the crown and going all the way down to the feet, drawing one large symbol to align the chakras and anchor the energy repatterning that has taken place.

· Continue with a normal treatment using all the level I symbols in sequence and following your inner guidance

· Offer a prayer of thanks for the healing that has taken place and acknowledge that it will continue.

Allergies

This technique can help bring relief of many allergy symptoms.

· Prayer of intention to release ego and activate all the Usui and Karuna Reiki energies, and to strengthen your light.

· Beam energy into the client's field with the intention of creating a healing link between the two of you.

· Draw the Usui power symbol down the front of the client's body starting at the crown and going all the way down to the feet, drawing one large symbol.

· Activate Zonar, Harth, Gnosa, Shanti, and Rama with one hand over the ascending heart chakra and one hand at the back of the heart chakra. Transmit the energy until the flow stops.

· Activate the Usui master symbol with Rama and Shanti and channel these frequencies into the entire etheric field until the flow stops.

· Continue with a normal treatment using all the level I symbols in sequence PLUS Shanti while also following your inner guidance

· Offer a prayer of thanks for the healing that has taken place and acknowledge that it will continue.

Anxiety

Here is a technique used to heal panic attacks or simply calm feelings of anxiety.

· Prayer of intention to release ego and activate all the Usui and Karuna Reiki energies, and to strengthen your light.

· Beam energy into the client's field with the intention of creating a healing link between the two of you.

· Activate Zonar, Gnosa, and Iava and Shanti, with one hand over the second chakra and one hand over the solar plexus. Transmit the energy until the flow stops.

· Activate the Usui master symbol and Rama and channel these frequencies into the entire etheric field until the flow stops.

· Continue with a normal treatment using all the level I symbols in sequence PLUS Shanti and following your inner guidance

· Offer a prayer of thanks for the healing that has taken place and acknowledge that it will continue.

Bleeding

A technique used to facilitate the control of bleeding in an emergency:

· Prayer of intention to release ego and activate all the Usui and Karuna Reiki energies, and to strengthen your light.

· Beam energy into the client's field to assess their energy and create a healing link.

· Activate Shanti to facilitate an increase in your clairvoyance and to relieve the recipient's pain.

· Activate the Usui Master symbol, Rama, and the Usui level II power symbol simultaneously and focus the energy with one hand held out in the etheric field over the heart chakra and one hand 2-3 inches above the point of injury. Transmit the energy until the bleeding stops. (If emergency help arrives, you can invoke the Usui distant healing symbol along with the symbols you are channeling and send the energy with the injured person.)

· Beam a combination of Karuna and Usui Reiki energy into the client's field until the healing is complete and seal as you would normally.

· Offer a prayer of thanks for the healing that has taken place and acknowledge that it will continue.

Cellular Memory Release

A technique used to clear cellular memory is described here.

· Prayer of intention to release ego and activate all the Usui and Karuna Reiki energies and to strengthen your light.

· Beam energy into the client's field with the intention of creating a healing link between the two of you.

· Activate Zonar, Halu, and Gnosa, with one hand over the second chakra and one hand over the causal chakra. Transmit the energy until the flow stops.

· Activate the Usui master symbol and Rama and channel these frequencies into the entire etheric field until the flow stops. Draw the Usui power symbol down the front of the body starting at the crown and going all the way down to the feet, drawing one large symbol to align the chakras and anchor the energy repatterning that has taken place.

· Continue with a normal treatment using all the level I symbols in sequence and following your inner guidance.

· Seal as you would normally.

· Offer a prayer of thanks for the healing that has taken place and acknowledge that it will continue.

Chakra Balancing

This technique can help clear, align and balance all the chakras simultaneously.

· Prayer of intention to release ego and activate all the Usui and Karuna Reiki energies and to strengthen your light.

· Beam energy into the client's field with the intention of creating a healing link between the two of you.

· Draw the Usui power symbol down the front of the client's body starting at the crown and going all the way down to the feet, drawing one large symbol.

· Activate Zonar, the Tibetan master symbol (if you know it), and Kriya and Rama, with one hand over the etheric heart chakra and one hand over the base chakra. Transmit the energy until the flow stops.

· Activate the Usui master symbol with Rama and channel these frequencies into the entire etheric field until the flow stops.

· Continue with a normal treatment using all the level I symbols in sequence PLUS Rama and following your inner guidance.

· Seal as you would normally.

· Offer a prayer of thanks for the healing that has taken place and acknowledge that it will continue.

Chemotherapy

It is possible to facilitate the positive effects of chemotherapy, by helping to neutralize toxicity and reduce side effects. This technique can help harmonize the client's body with this very strong medication. This is most effective if done a minimum of four times immediately prior to the chemotherapy treatment, preferably once each day for four days prior.

· Prayer of intention to release ego and activate all the Usui and Karuna Reiki' energies and to strengthen your light.

· Beam energy into the client's field with the intention of creating a healing link between the two of you.

· Draw the Usui power symbol down the front of the client's body starting at the crown and going all the way down to the feet, drawing one large symbol.

· Activate Zonar, Halu, Harth, Rama and the Usui power and master symbols with one hand over the area of the liver and one hand under the body in the area of the adrenals; transmit the energy until the flow stops.

· Activate the Usui master symbol with Rama and channel these frequencies into the entire etheric field until the flow stops. Then activate Shanti and transmit this symbol alone into the etheric field.

· Continue with a normal treatment using all the level I symbols in sequence PLUS Rama and following your inner guidance.

· Seal as you would normally.

Offer a prayer of thanks for the healing that has taken place and acknowledge that it will continue.

Delusion and Denial

A technique used to heal an attitude of denial or bring a clearer sense of current reality is as follows:

· Prayer of intention to release ego and activate all the Usui and Karuna Reiki' energies and to strengthen your light.

· Beam energy into the client's field with the intention of creating a healing link between the two of you.

· Activate Zonar, Halu, Iava, Harth and the Usui mental and emotional symbol. With one hand at the back of the head at the base of the skull and one hand over the second chakra. Transmit the energy until the flow stops. Move one hand over the solar plexus and one hand over the base chakra and continue to channel Zonar, Halu, Iava, Harth and the Usui mental and emotional symbol until the flow stops.

· Activate the Usui master symbol and Rama and channel these frequencies into the entire etheric field until the flow stops. Draw the Usui power symbol down the front of the body starting at the crown and going all the way down to the feet, drawing one large symbol to align the chakras and anchor the energy repatterning that has taken place.

· Continue with a normal treatment using all the level I symbols in sequence and following your inner guidance

· Seal as you would normally.

· Offer a prayer of thanks for the healing that has taken place and acknowledge that it will continue.

Developing Healthy Habits

This technique can help increase the vibration of love for self and facilitate the development of healthy habits, such as eating properly or exercising:

· Prayer of intention to release ego and activate all the Usui and Karuna Reiki energies and to strengthen your light.

· Beam energy into the client's field with the intention of creating a healing link between the two of you.

· Activate Zonar, Harth, Gnosa, Iava and the Usui mental and emotional symbol. With one hand at the back of the head at the base of the skull and one hand over the brow chakra. Transmit the energy until the flow stops. Move one hand over the solar plexus and one hand over the heart chakra and continue to channel Zonar, Harth, Gnosa Iava, and the Usui mental and emotional symbol until the flow stops.

· Activate the Usui master symbol and Rama and channel these frequencies over the base chakra until the flow stops. Draw the Usui power symbol down the front of the body, starting at the crown and going all the way down to the feet, drawing one large symbol to align the chakras and anchor the energy repatterning that has taken place.

· Continue with a normal treatment using all the level I symbols in sequence and following your inner guidance.

· Seal as you would normally.

· Offer a prayer of thanks for the healing that has taken place and acknowledge that it will continue.

Generational Healing –
Healing Our Ancestors and Our Future

Many of the issues that we have to heal are genetically coded into our consciousness and our actual DNA from our ancestors. This technique can help send healing energy back in time to our ancestors to help them heal, bring the healed energy into our bodies, and also time capsule it for future generations.

Channel healing and joy to your ancestors and allow the essence of their transformation to flow into your life and the lives of future generations.

This is the technique that I have found to be helpful personally:

· Prayer of intention to release ego and activate all the Usui and Karuna Reiki· energies and to strengthen your light.

· Hold the intention of creating a healing link between you, your ancestors and the Archangels, Gabriel, Michael, Raphael, Camiel and Zophkiel. Give thanks that the healing energy flows to you, your guides, masters, your ancestors, and future generations for the highest good of all, and with soul permission of those willing to heal.

· Invoke the Usui distant healing symbol, Zonar, Halu, Harth, Gnosa, Iava and the Usui mental/emotional symbol with the intention of creating a bridge of light through the generations that came before you and those that are yet to come. When you feel this link you may begin to feel the presence of spiritual guides or of specific ancestors who come forward to participate in the healing. Bring in any other healing energy that you feel guided to work with. Then simply let the energy flow.

· Channel energy and meditate for as long as it feels appropriate, be aware of anything you feel, sense or think. Often messages will come to assist you in understanding any particular genetic coding that you may be holding onto that is ready to be released.

· When the healing/meditation session feels complete, give thanks to the Divine, your guides, and masters. Also thank the ancestors and the future generations for sharing in the healing and acknowledge that the healing will continue.

· Activate the Usui master symbol and Rama and channel these frequencies over the base chakra until the flow stops. Draw the Usui power symbol down the front of the body starting at the crown and going all the way down to the feet, drawing one large symbol to align the chakras and anchor the energy repatterning that has taken place.

· Do this as often as you can until you notice shifts in your thoughts, feelings, body, or circumstances. I strongly encourage you to do this daily for 21 days for the most magnificent results.

Karmic Issues

A technique used to facilitate karmic healing is described here. The client should be sitting during this session.

· Prayer of intention to release ego and activate all the Usui and Karuna Reiki energies and to strengthen your light.

· Beam energy into the client's field with the intention of creating a healing link between you, the client and Archangel Gabriel, using the Usui distant healing symbol.

· Activate Zonar and Halu to facilitate karmic healing, and the Usui Master symbol, and Rama simultaneously. Beam the energy with one hand held out in the energy field over the front of the etheric heart and one hand at the back of the etheric heart. Transmit the energy until the flow stops.

· Continue with a normal treatment using all the level I symbols in sequence and following your inner guidance.

· Seal as you would normally.

· Offer a prayer of thanks for the healing that has taken place and acknowledge that it will continue.

Note: You can do this technique on yourself by telepathically projecting the symbols into the positions described and placing your hands on your physical heart center and channeling the energy until it stops flowing.

Mental Focus and Grounding

When we have a busy mind or are faced with many tasks to accomplish it is very easy to become unfocused or ungrounded. This technique can help us create priorities and call our energies back into our body so we can be more productive.

· Prayer of intention to release ego and activate all the Usui and Karuna Reiki® energies and to strengthen your light.

· Beam energy into the client's field with the intention of creating a healing link between yourself and the client.

· Activate Zonar, Kriya, Rama, and the Usui master symbol and beam the energy with both hands over the solar plexus. Transmit the energy until the flow stops.

· Continue with a normal treatment using all the level I symbols in sequence and following your inner guidance.

· Seal as you would normally.

· Offer a prayer of thanks for the healing that has taken place and acknowledge that it will continue.

Physical Injuries/Emergencies

This is technique used for supporting the healing of a broken bone, burns and stings/insect bites:

· Prayer of intention to release ego, activate the Usui and Karuna Reiki energies and strengthen your light.

· Beam energy into the client's field, when possible have others help.

· Activate Shanti to facilitate an increase in your clairvoyance and to relieve the recipient's pain.

· Chant Kriya, followed by Rama. Chant them in rapid succession with intensity for approximately 3-5 minutes.

· Activate Halu for cellular memory release and to facilitate aura clearing while working in the emotional and mental bodies until the release is complete.

· Beam a combination of Karuna and Usui Reiki energy into the client's field until the flow stops and seal as you would normally.

· Offer a prayer of thanks for the healing that has taken place and acknowledge that it will continue.

I have had an opportunity to use this technique several times with similar results. I feel that it would be helpful in any emergency situation where physical healing is needed, and Reiki can be administered soon after the injury happens or illness begins.

Resistance to Healing

Sometimes we have a resistance to healing and as a defense mechanism we create an etheric armor around our energy field that makes it difficult for healing energy to penetrate and help us.

If you or one of your clients seems to have this resistance, the first thing you need to do is determine whether you, or your client, are _ready and willing_ to heal.

The session might go like this:

· Prayer of intention to release ego and activate all the Usui and Karuna Reiki` energies and to strengthen your light.

· Beam energy into the client's field with the intention of creating a healing link between the two of you.

· Draw the Usui mental and emotional symbol over the front of the client's heart and solar plexus area (draw only one symbol covering both areas)

· Ask the client to repeat the following affirmation:

> "I AM ready and willing to heal."
> "I release all resistance to healing."
> "I release all fear of healing"
> "I accept complete healing now."

· Activate Zonar, Harth, Iava, Kriya and Rama, with one hand over the solar plexus and one hand over the base chakra. Transmit the energy until the flow stops. Then move one hand over the second chakra and one hand over the heart. Continue to channel Zonar, Harth, Iava, Kriya and Rama until the flow stops.

· Continue with a normal treatment using all the level I symbols in sequence PLUS Shanti and following your inner guidance.

· Seal as you would normally.

· Offer a prayer of thanks for the healing that has taken place and acknowledge that it will continue.

Spiritual Growth

This technique is used to facilitate our spiritual growth by helping us stay focused on our path.

· Prayer of intention to release ego and activate all the Usui and Karuna Reiki® energies and to strengthen your light.

· Beam energy into the client's field with the intention of creating a healing link between you, the client and Archangel Michael, using the Usui distant healing symbol.

· Activate Gnosa, Kriya Iava, Shanti and the Usui master symbol and beam the energy with one hand over the solar plexus and one hand over the heart. Transmit the energy until the flow stops.

· Continue with a normal treatment using all the level I symbols in sequence and following your inner guidance.

· Seal as you would normally.

· Offer a prayer of thanks for the healing that has taken place and acknowledge that it will continue.

Karuna Symbols and Our Spiritual Guides

In the section entitled "Recognizing Our Spiritual Guides" which concerns working with our guides, I mentioned methods to connect with the Angels, Masters and guides that utilize the Karuna Reiki symbols. Let's review that process now.

First of all, let's look at which symbols can facilitate our connection with the Archangels and the Divine Temples.

Divine Temple	Divine Purpose	Karuna Reiki Symbols
Auriel Compassion	Universal compassion, Nature, Earth	Usui distance/power **Harth, Iava, Kriya**
Zadkiel Creation	Manifestation, visualization, Creativity	Usui distance/Master **Gnosa, Shanti, Rama**
Michael Truth	Strength, protection, truth, Balance of light	Usui distance/Master **Harth, Iava, Rama**
Raphael Love	Healing, love, Emotional experience	Distance/mental-emotional **Harth, Shanti**
Alteal Peace	Peace, evolution, Dimensional awareness	Usui distance/Master **Zonar, Halu, Harth,** **Gnosa, Shanti**
Gabriel Knowledge	Teaching, sound, Communication, alchemy	Usui distance/Master **Gnosa, Harth, Iava, Rama**
Zophkiel Beauty/Sight	Beauty, artistic expression, Divine law and order	Usui distance/Master **Gnosa, Kriya, Iava,** **Harth, Rama**
Camiel Light	Light, power, prayer, energy	Distance/Power/Master **Harth, Rama, Kriya,** **Iava, Shanti**
Haniel Divine Purpose Personal	Magnificence, Aligning with Divine power/purpose	Usui distance/Master **Gnosa, Iava, Harth,** **Shanti, Rama**

You will notice that the Usui distance symbol is used first in each instance. It is possible to connect without the Usui symbols, however my experience indicates that use of the Usui energy enhances the use of

Karuna Reiki. Conversely, Karuna Reiki enhances work done with Usui Reiki. They are both great healing gifts that we have been blessed with.

The Usui distance symbol helps to lay an energetic pathway, or a bridge of light from the light of the Divine within us to the light of the Divine within our spiritual guides. This link facilitates clear communication.

The order the symbols are printed here is not the only way you can work with them. Experiment with rearranging the order and see if it alters your experience.

An example of a technique to link with one of the Archangel Realms follows.

Communicating with the Archangel Realms

This technique is used to facilitate our ability to communicate with the Archangel Realms. This example is connecting with the realm of Michael.

Michael	Strength, protection, truth,	Usui distance & Master,	
Truth	Balance of light	Harth, Iava, Rama	

Michael	Strength, protection, truth,	Cobalt Blue/Yellow	Azurite/Citrine/Pearl
Truth	Balance of light	Solar Plexus	Amber/Tanzanite

· Prayer of intention to release ego and activate all the Usui and Karuna Reiki energies and to strengthen your light.

· Beam energy into your solar plexus and/or a piece of azurite, citrine, pearl, amber or tanzanite. Hold the intention of creating a healing link between yourself, and Archangel Michael, using the Usui distant healing and Master symbol.

· Activate Harth, Iava, and Rama. Beam this energy with one hand over the solar plexus and one hand over the heart. Ask questions or meditate and transmit the energy until the flow stops.

· Offer a prayer of thanks for the communication that has taken place. Acknowledge your gratitude for the strength to act upon the guidance you have discerned is right for you. (Remember you are personally responsible for all the choices made in your life)

Journaling and Spiritual Communication

I have found journaling my Karuna meditations to be a key element in facilitating spiritual communication with my higherself, the angelic beings, masters, and God. In working with my journal I have come to understand the seamlessness that exists between the spiritual realms and our physical existence.

We will be exploring the Divine Temples in the next section of this book. Journaling these experiences can assist you in expanding your sentient awareness through repeated practice and reflection on your meditation process.

I have included some journal pages for your use as you explore the Divine Temples. One page is for notes, and another is left blank so that you have plenty of room to draw or color, if you are so inspired.

Make notations in your journal of any sensory experiences you had, i.e. what did you feel, see, or hear? Did any particular thoughts arise. Did you see any symbols?

How did you feel when you started the session? Were you tired, rested, stressed, calm, angry, happy, etc. How did you feel when you completed the session? Record, your physical, mental, emotional and spiritual responses in your journal. What is going on in your life that is of particular importance at this time?

How are you relating to your family, friends, co-workers, and yourself? If any relationships are particularly difficult, or good, make a note of that. As you begin to hold more light, you will notice the energetic exchange between you and those you regularly relate with may change. You will become more likely to attract better, higher forms of relationships, transform existing ones, or move on to healthier situations.

What are your personal goals for growth, healing and inner peace? Write them down, and watch how the energy helps you move closer to manifesting the goals that are truly in alignment with your life purpose.

Have FUN with these meditations and with your journal . . . be BOLD. You can write in your journal, draw in it ... color ... there are no rules ... express yourself! Grow! EnJOY!

Experiencing the Divine Temples

This technique is used to facilitate our ability to experience the Divine Temples. This example assists our travel upon the inner planes to the Divine Temple of Love.

Raphael	Healing, love,	Usui distance & mental-emotional	
Love	Emotional experience	Harth, Shanti	

Raphael	Healing, love,	Iridescent Green/Pink	Pink Kunzite/Muscovite
Love	Emotional experience	Heart, Sacral	Chrysoprase/Apophylite

Have materials ready to journal or draw if you are guided to do so at the end of this alignment session. Pages are provided to write and draw your experiences.

· Prayer of intention to release ego and activate all the Usui and Karuna Reiki` energies and to strengthen your light.

· Activate the Usui distance and mental/emotional symbol and beam this energy into your heart/or a piece of pink kunzite, muscovite, chrysoprase, or apophylite. Hold the intention of creating a healing link between yourself, and Archangel Raphael and to travel to the Divine Temple of Love.

· Give thanks that your connection with the Realm of Archangel Raphael is fully activated in this moment and you are assisted in aligning with the Temple of Love. Activate Harth, and Shanti. Beam this energy with one hand over the heart and one hand over the sacral chakra. Continue beaming until the flow stops.

Begin the journey per the illustration and description that follows. . .

A Journey to the Divine Temples

1. Be aware of your sacred heart, ascending heart and soul vision centers. (The sacred heart is slightly behind and below your physical heart, the ascending heart is behind the thymus between the heart and throat, and the soul vision center is concentrated in the center of the head behind the third eye, but slightly lower.)

2. Visualize Archangel Raphael as a great being of light sitting in front of you. Be aware of his sacred heart, ascending heart and soul vision centers.

3. Send a beam of silver out the front of your sacred heart, as Archangel Raphael does the same, and the beams connect.

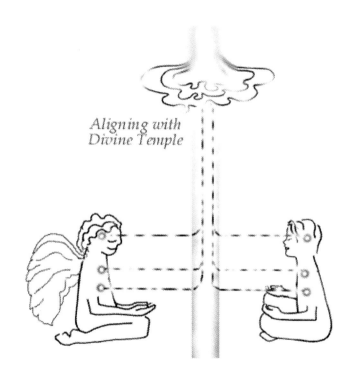

*Aligning with
Divine Temple*

4. Send a beam of golden light out the front of your ascending heart as Archangel Raphael does the same and the beams connect.

5. Send a beam of pearlescent, opalescent, shimmering white light out from your soul vision center, until it connects with a similar beam from Archangel Raphael.

6. When this connection is made and light is flowing back and forth fluidly between the two of you, focus on your soul vision center in the center of your head, behind your third eye. See pulsating white iridescent light there. As you are doing this, Archangel Raphael is doing the same thing and a column of pearlescent light is forming in between the two of you. This is a huge column of light and you feel the three energy centers active and connected to it.

7. A beam of light from your soul vision center is connecting with this column of light that appears to flow from the heart of the Earth up into the heart of God. Your (you and Archangel Raphael) soul vision centers blend and together your consciousness is rising higher and higher. You are entering the essence of the Divine Temple of Love. This is a place where there is no form...only light...you connect here to the actual energetic essence of the Divine Temple of Love. You will feel what Divine Love is. Allow yourself to embrace it.

8. Breathe this essence into every atom and cell of your being. Exhale out into your energy body. Inhale and exhale while focusing on your intention to integrate the full essence of Divine Love in your body, mind and etheric field.

9. Stay here for a while allowing yourself to absorb this energy. You are different here . . . you too are all light and no form.

10. When you feel ready, consciously draw the light from your soul vision center back into your head, and allow the light to permeate your entire being.

11. Gently disconnect the golden beam of light and draw it into yourself, and let it blend with the iridescent soul light.

12. Do the same with the beam of silver light.

13. Repeat the breathing technique that you started with.

14. Focus on the energies swirling in your body feeling them permeate every single cell of your body. You are actually breathing this energy in from your etheric field, anchoring it into your body, and allowing it to flow down into the earth to ground the vibrations of Divine Love and Universal Compassion in yourself, and into the Earth.

Take a moment to offer a prayer of thanks for the healing and alignment that has taken place. Open your journal and begin to express yourself by writing or drawing.

Note: You can adapt this basic technique to align with any of the Divine Temples.

Journey to Divine Temples - Journal Notes

Divine Temple of : Compassion, Love, Light, Truth, Peace,
Beauty/Sight, Creation, Knowledge, Divine Purpose (circle one)

_____

_____

_____

_____

_____

_____

_____

_____

_____

_____

_____

_____

_____

_____

_____

_____

Divine Temples - Journey Doodles & Visions

Journey to Divine Temples - Journal Notes

Divine Temple of : Compassion, Love, Light, Truth, Peace,
Beauty/Sight, Creation, Knowledge, Divine Purpose (circle one)

_____

_____

_____

_____

_____

_____

_____

_____

_____

_____

_____

_____

_____

_____

_____

_____

Divine Temples - Journey Doodles & Visions

Journey to Divine Temples - Journal Notes

Divine Temple of: Compassion, Love, Light, Truth, Peace,
Beauty/Sight, Creation, Knowledge, Divine Purpose (circle one)

Divine Temples - Journey Doodles & Visions

Journey to Divine Temples - Journal Notes

Divine Temple of: Compassion, Love, Light, Truth, Peace,
Beauty/Sight, Creation, Knowledge, Divine Purpose (circle one)

_____

_____

_____

_____

_____

_____

_____

_____

_____

_____

_____

_____

_____

_____

_____

Divine Temples - Journey Doodles & Visions

Journey to Divine Temples - Journal Notes

Divine Temple of : Compassion, Love, Light, Truth, Peace,
Beauty/Sight, Creation, Knowledge, Divine Purpose (circle one)

Divine Temples - Journey Doodles & Visions

Journey to Divine Temples - Journal Notes

Divine Temple of: Compassion, Love, Light, Truth, Peace,
Beauty/Sight, Creation, Knowledge, Divine Purpose (circle one)

_____

_____

_____

_____

_____

_____

_____

_____

_____

_____

_____

_____

_____

_____

_____

_____

Divine Temples - Journey Doodles & Visions

Journey to Divine Temples - Journal Notes

Divine Temple of: Compassion, Love, Light, Truth, Peace, Beauty/Sight, Creation, Knowledge, Divine Purpose (circle one)

_____

_____

_____

_____

_____

_____

_____

_____

_____

_____

_____

_____

_____

_____

_____

_____

_____

Divine Temples - Journey Doodles & Visions

Journey to Divine Temples - Journal Notes

Divine Temple of: Compassion, Love, Light, Truth, Peace,
Beauty/Sight, Creation, Knowledge, Divine Purpose (circle one)

_____

_____

_____

_____

_____

_____

_____

_____

_____

_____

_____

_____

_____

_____

_____

_____

_____

Divine Temples - Journey Doodles & Visions

Journey to Divine Temples - Journal Notes

Divine Temple of: Compassion, Love, Light, Truth, Peace, Beauty/Sight, Creation, Knowledge, Divine Purpose (circle one)

Divine Temples - Journey Doodles & Visions

A Healing Emergency in Hawaii

One of the many wonderful characteristics of Karuna Reiki® is its inherent potential to increase our ability to discern spiritual guidance. This can be very valuable to help develop new, effective healing techniques.

As we know, Reiki is spiritually guided life force energy. The integration of Karuna Reiki into a treatment has helped activate new channels for the guiding energies to share techniques that may be unique to a particular situation. After working with these new techniques they often evolve so that they can be used in many circumstances.

During a retreat in Hawaii I was offered a technique to help one of the participants heal from an injury. This student, along with several others made a journey to the volcano park in their off hours late one evening. It was very dark, and the volcanic rock, though beautiful, can be treacherous to walk on. On this evening it was especially humid which created very moist night air, causing the rock to be slippery. She fell and broke her left arm and "injured" the right one. With the help of her Reiki friends, she visited the emergency room. Her left arm was x-rayed, but her right one was not. It was confirmed that the left arm was broken.

By the next morning she was experiencing excruciating pain and swelling in her right hand. During the morning healing circle and meditation the guides prompted me to ask the class to help her and we performed a group healing session. At the end of a session I was given a message that, when she returned to the mainland and saw her doctor, she would receive a miracle. In that moment I felt the specific vibration of the Shanti, which helps enhance clairvoyance vibrating in my throat, third eye and crown chakras.

I experienced an x-ray like flash of vision in which I actually saw inside her hand, saw a broken bone and watched as if I were viewing a video being fast-forwarded. I was shown a vision of the bone healing very quickly as it was "rewoven" by ribbons of light. This triggered a knowing that, although the hospital had not x-rayed the right hand, it was broken. This would account for the extreme swelling and severe pain also.

Of course, because Reiki practitioners do not diagnose, and because I didn't want to empower that thought, I didn't say anything. I simply focused on the image of the hand healing itself. Later that day I was working with the Karuna Reiki students in our class. We invited our friend into the class for a group treatment. As the session began it became immediately apparent that we should incorporate chanting. A few of us worked with her "hands on" while others beamed and chanted.

As the energy increased and the vibration grew higher, the guiding energies began to prompt me to create a special chant, combining Kriya for physical healing and Rama for harmonizing the upper and lower chakras. These were chanted with intensity in rapid succession.

The effect was that it caused unhealthy energy to lift from the physical body and settle in a "pocket" between the mental and emotional etheric bodies. Then Halu, which facilitates cellular memory release and "psychic" surgery, was activated. As I held my hand out in her etheric field, in the area of the pocket of dense energy, it began to shake and vibrate uncontrollably and a brilliant beam of light began to flow into the area.

Suddenly the area of density burst into what appeared to be thousands of particles of pure white light. Her energy field became calm; the geometric patterns contained within it were regular and smooth. The healing was complete. The next morning the pain and swelling were greatly reduced.

In talking with the student after we returned from Hawaii I learned that she did indeed receive her miracle, which was promised that day during the healing circle. She told me that she knew the right hand had been broken, and when she had it x-rayed on the mainland, it was nearly healed with only minor bruising.

It was from this experience that the technique for healing injuries and emergency situations has evolved.

Unconditional Reiki - Free Yourself to Heal

There are so many wonderful Reiki and Karuna Reiki stories about miracles. However there are also many times when we question whether the energy is working. I receive questions from practitioners all around the world, all asking the same questions; "Why don't I get results with Reiki like the people in your stories? What am I doing wrong?"

The answer to those questions is "You are doing nothing wrong!"

We do need to understand there are three core elements involved in healing; fear, trust and release. When we learn to do our healing work fearlessly, trust it completely, and step out of the way by releasing all attachment to outcome, we open the door for miracles; we can do nothing wrong. This is unconditional Reiki. This is how we free ourselves to heal and be healed.

When we begin to use Karuna Reiki it becomes even more important for us to free ourselves from expectations and fear. If we try to set limits on the energy, we restrict the flow and it is more difficult for the guides to work with us.

Fear can enter into our sessions in many ways. We can fear that we are doing something wrong, or that the client doesn't feel anything, that our hands are not warm enough, or simply that it may not work. The first step in healing these fears requires remembering that Reiki is defined as "spiritually guided" life force energy. It is infinite wisdom and healing love that knows exactly what the recipient needs. Because Reiki is infinitely wise, it can *never* cause harm.

The only "rule" with Reiki is to "Let it Be" and know that it is perfect. I am very blessed that my teachers taught me that Reiki never causes harm, before I was told of the other *"Reiki Rules"*. After I had become a completely trusting practitioner, I was told to never Reiki a broken bone before it has been set because it might heal incorrectly, and to never Reiki a burn because the heat will make it worse.

I am thankful I was not warned of these things before, on a wintry day in southern Indiana, I had the opportunity to hold my Reiki hands around my friend's broken ankle (she refused emergency room treatment) and saw the bone set before my eyes.

I am thankful that when I burned my hand on a 450 degree pan handle, I hadn't yet been told that Reiki shouldn't be used, because I found immediate relief from the cooling effect Reiki had on my blistered hand, which completely healed in hours.

You see, I was fearless and completely trusting when I opened for Reiki to flow through, and then I just let it be. If you truly believe that Reiki is spiritually guided life force energy, which can only be used for the highest good of all concerned, then you can set your fears and your ego aside and channel Reiki in its purest form.

This makes the next steps easy, trust and release. Trust the intelligence of the energy to know what's best and to do it. Know that this is done and give thanks for the blessings. The only thing left to do is wait to see how the healing manifests.

Let me give you an example of a client, Debra. She came to me knowing nothing of Reiki; all she knew was she had been guided to my door. She had been diagnosed with type III breast cancer and a few weeks earlier had a mastectomy. There are many stories within her case, but let's focus now on non-attachment to outcome.

Debra was to receive chemotherapy for four months prior to a bone marrow transplant, which she had been told was her only chance for survival.

We had been giving her Reiki and Karuna Reiki to strengthen her and to neutralize side effects of chemotherapy, while maximizing its benefits. She asked me to include in my prayer that she not lose her hair. I told her that I couldn't do this. I said "I know Reiki will minimize the side effects, but I don't feel it is right to limit our potential by asking for this specifically."

Our prayer was that Reiki help the perfect healing take place for the highest good of all concerned, and that God's Will be done through us.

Debra did so well with her first round of chemotherapy she found herself sending Reiki to the other patients on her floor, because they were having a much more difficult time than she was.

Debra lost her hair. However, the lady who sold her a wig referred her to a friend who knew a lot about her type of cancer. This friend referred her to a special program at a hospital out of state that has a much higher success rate than the hospital she had planned to attend. The new hospital encouraged family involvement, and her doctor even encouraged her to continue with Reiki.

I know, with every atom of my being, Reiki's infinite wisdom chose for her to lose her hair so this connection could be made. Debra is just one example of how wise Reiki truly is.

Healing Is Different Than Curing.

Reiki produces beautiful results, and we only need to be open to the many forms it takes.

I have worked for several months with a woman who has fibromyalgia. Because of her chronic pain, she learned to suppress many of her feelings. When she is on the Reiki table she rarely "feels" anything happening. However, she processes quite a bit in her dream state after Reiki treatments and is aware that she feels better hours, or days later.

Her treatment is requiring deep fears and attitudes to be changed, and she is able to process these changes only gradually. However, Reiki is healing her a little at a time and I have absolute faith that she is healing in the most perfect way.

Reiki helped my grandmother leave this plane when her 92-year old body was ready to release her spirit. However, this did not happen until Reiki communicated what needed to be done. This wonderful woman was in a self-imposed coma, after consciously choosing to die. She remained comatose for weeks, with only fluids to sustain her.

I sat by my grandmother's bed day after day, administering Reiki. Then one very memorable day Reiki began to speak to me and gave me words to pray for her. She had some unfinished business, Reiki told me why she was hanging on, and Reiki delivered a beautiful prayer from my lips.

As soon as the prayer was finished, my grandmother opened her eyes, looked right into mine, and asked, "Who are all those people with the red candles?" Reiki replied...."Those are the angels who have come to take you back to Jesus." She closed her eyes, sighed, and the first wisps of life force began to leave her body. She left this plane peacefully . . . thanks to Reiki, the love of God.

This was not a cure, but a true healing.

As Reiki practitioners we think of the energy as unconditional love. To produce the best possible results we must also unconditionally love Reiki. By allowing it to flow in its purest form and completely trusting it to do what's best, we truly serve in the highest possible way as instruments of peace and healing.

Allow yourself to practice unconditional Reiki and free yourself to heal!

Karuna Reiki® and Healing with Sound

Usui Reiki Treatment for Body and Mind

"Just for today, do not anger

Do not worry and be filled with gratitude

Devote yourself to your work and be kind to people

Every morning and every evening join your hands in prayer

Pray these words with your heart and
<u>chant</u> these words with your mouth"

~ The Original Reiki Ideals ~

Mt. Kurama Chanting Inspiration

In September of 1997, Arjava Petter invited William Rand and myself to Japan. The purpose of this journey was to research the true history of Reiki, which we did. However, from a personal, spiritual perspective, the experience was about much more than uncovering historical facts on Reiki.

So much happened to me during this journey I could probably write an entire book on the experience. However, for the purpose of this topic I would like to focus on my inspirations from Mt. Kurama.

As most of you know, Mt. Kurama is the sacred mountain in Japan where Usui Sensei first discovered Reiki. It is about a one-hour ride by train from the city of Kyoto.

There are many sacred mountains in Japan and each has a specific meaning, spiritual purpose and animal spirit or totem.

The totem animal of Mt. Kurama is the tiger. As we stood at the foot of this magnificent mountain next to the sculpture of the spiral tiger, Yuki, our guide, explained that tiger represents the spirit of change. He said, "When Japanese people want their energy changed, they come to this mountain."

That information caused me to reflect on why Usui Sensei chose this particular mountain for his quest. Remembering that he was having some difficulties in his life at the time, it now seemed very logical that he would choose Mt. Kurama.

Many magnificent things happened to us on that mountain, beginning with an awareness of three spheres of light that seemed to be accompanying us everywhere we went. These spheres were emanating an incredibly loving vibration.

One particularly memorable experience was when Yuki obtained special permission for the three of us to enter the Honden Temple. We sat quietly on the floor waiting for the priest. During these silent moments I was so very aware of the sacredness of this space, as well as the presence of three great beings of light.

When the priest entered, he silently and energetically acknowledged the three of us. He then began his sacred ceremony. A portion of his ritual involved the sounding of chimes, bells and chanting. Among the many sounds he chanted were the names of the Usui master symbol and two of the Karuna symbols.

The vibration in the temple continued to rise with his chants. At one point I felt as if we were levitating about 2 feet off the floor. I don't think we were actually physically levitating, but etherically I know we were. It felt as if we had entered some sort of chamber of light. I suddenly became aware that from somewhere in front and above us, beams of different colored light were shining into the three of us. Each of us received transmissions of this colored light that were unique and that entered different chakras.

Next the beams of light moved beside and then behind us. At one point I saw something similar to a double helix of rainbow light flowing through William and Yuki, and I felt and partially saw the same thing happening to me. I felt magnificent shifts in my energy that created a very deep sense of peace, but also euphoria.

This phenomenal display of light eventually stopped, and everything in the temple was very quiet and peaceful.

When the priest completed the ceremony, with a deep sense of gratitude we continued our hike up the mountain.

I was again aware of the three spheres of light that sometimes seemed to follow us and at other times appeared to be guiding us.

When we arrived at the top of the mountain it was as if we had stepped into another world. The forest was magnificent. A shrine to Mao-son, who many Japanese people believe to be the salvation and spirit of the Earth, offered shelter for those who wished to pray and meditate inside.

We eventually went our separate ways to have the opportunity to pray and meditate in solitude.

I was inspired to pray, meditate, and send Reiki as I sat next to a tree with a spiral trunk. I first was so very aware of the wind blowing through the trees and the sounds of running water, but soon the sounds faded into the background.

I sent Reiki to Usui Sensei and all the people who have ever practiced Reiki in the past, practice it today, or will practice Reiki in the future. I sent Reiki to Gaia, our earth mother. Gradually I became aware of sounds that seemed to be coming from in between the wind, they were chants! The first chant I heard was Om Shanti Gaia, I then heard a variety of chants combining the names of all the Usui Reiki symbols, as well as some of the Karuna symbols. I thought of the Reiki Ideals, particularly this portion:

"Pray these words with your heart and
<u>chant</u> these words with your mouth"

In that moment I *knew* what this statement meant. I felt Usui Sensei's presence as if he were acknowledging my inner knowing that there is incredible healing power in the sounds associated with the symbols.

I sat under that spiral tree on this sacred mountain and chanted softly for a long time.

Karuna Reiki Chanting

You may recall the story I shared with you earlier in which I said the name Avalokiteshvara translates to Maha Karuna., or "great compassion". According to the <u>Shambala Dictionary of Buddhism and Zen</u> there is another translation, "*Sound that Illumines the World*".

Every culture from ancient times to modern day has expressed the power of music and sound in some form. Sound is a vehicle for alchemical change and thus for healing.

When we first started teaching Karuna Reiki, chanting was not a part of the program at all. However, within days of "meeting" Avalokiteshvara we found ourselves being guided to chant Karuna sounds in our healing sessions. What we found was that it greatly intensified the energy and there were often major shifts for the recipient. When we realized how important this was to the healing power, we prayed, meditated, asked for guidance; and ultimately incorporated chanting into Karuna Reiki training.

Our voice carries a vibration merging us with healing light that transcends time and space, moving us into the time continuum. Chanting brings us instantaneously in to the moment of "now". The now moment is the only place from which we can touch into the resonance of the past or the future.

When we chant or sing, our soul recognizes the true essence of the words or tones through the vibrations resounding in our body. Chanting allows spirit to flow in and expand the mind.

It is our throat chakra that blends the in-breath and the out-breath or the energies of heaven and earth. When we inhale we breathe in the essence of the heavens, and when we exhale we connect heaven with the earth. Blending the energy in this way creates wholeness in our physical being.

We also blend masculine and feminine energies when we chant. We connect with Divine intelligence through our intuitive (feminine) self with the in-breath, and we bring forth or manifest sound with our masculine energy on the out-breath.

Chanting creates specific energetic tapestries of sound as vowels and consonants are woven into repetitive patterns.

The cellular healing abilities inherent in Karuna Reiki energy are enhanced by chanting. This is because each of our cells resonates and their resonance is affected by sound and light.

When we chant it is helpful to know that the core or the power is in the vowel, and consonants serve as the conduit for the sound to flow through. Regardless of what language one speaks, the vowels consistently carry their own sacred resonance.

In _The Development of Modern English_ by Robinson and Cassidy, vowels are defined as "musical tones made by a regular vibration of the vocal cords and modified by varying the shape and size of the resonance chamber." The modifications spoken of here directly affect the power the vowel has to heal.

The power of vowels can be felt by doing an exercise of intoning (inner chanting or toning). Simply focus on the breath, and on the in-breath place your awareness in a corresponding area of the body while intoning the vowel that opens that area. For example, breathe in, focus on your heart and silently tone an "A" (as in day). Repeat this a few times and feel your heart center expand.

Here is a chart of the vowel body relationships:

Chakra	Vowel	Sound
Heart	A	day
Throat	A	cat
Solar Plexus	A	paw
Brow	E	see
Crown	E	see
Throat	E	met
Mouth of God**	I	sky
Throat	I	in
Creative	O	home
Solar Plexus	O	on
Base	U	tune
Throat	U	up

**The base of the skull

When we combine chanting and toning with Karuna Reiki® energy, both the power of the vowel and the qualities of the Karuna healing frequencies blend to create varying effects. They can be intoned, or chanted aloud. Both methods create unique frequencies.

Normally Karuna chanting is guided by the Reiki energy, allowing us to simply channel the sounds that will be most helpful in any particular situation.

Chanting is simply another way of creating a pathway of flow for the energy to travel. Chanting during healing sessions is as beneficial for the chanter as it is for the recipient of the session.

One of the best ways to learn the true nature of Karuna Reiki® is to meditate and allow your consciousness to merge totally with the light and sound of Karuna.

When we integrate Karuna chanting into our lives, we expand the corridors within our hearts and minds to receive greater levels of Divine inspiration. Divine Love and Universal compassion fuel our creativity, and we are empowered to birth new forms, ideas, and creations through our personal expression of Being.

Karuna Reiki® with Drumming and Crystal Bowls

There are many ways to incorporate sound with Reiki energy to facilitate healing. We have developed healing techniques that incorporate Karuna Reiki® with shamanic drumming and crystal singing bowls.

These techniques, in addition to having powerful healing effects, help us comprehend from an experiential perspective, the intensity and sacred power of sound and light that can be channeled through musical instruments.

Although these techniques require training, I felt I should mention them here so that it reminds you that the methods in which we can use these energies are limitless.

Quality Reiki and Karuna Reiki® Training

It is well known in the Reiki community that Usui Reiki is taught in many different ways and often students are unsure if they have received adequate training. Much of my life is dedicated to helping other Reiki Masters become confident, successful teachers. There are many wonderful teachers available. However, as in all professions, there are some people who are more dedicated to honest, ethical practice than others.

It saddens me when I meet students who received drastically abbreviated Reiki training and have no access to their teacher after class. I find this disheartening because these students have little or no confidence in Reiki. They don't know what to do with the energy, what it is or how to use it. Often they were given drawings of the symbols, but have no idea what they are for. The teachers at the ICRT frequently have students who received such training come to us asking for help.

What good does it do to receive Reiki training and then not have the confidence to use it? I feel it is important for students to know how to apply Reiki to every single aspect of their life.

When choosing a qualified Usui Reiki Master as your teacher, it is a good idea to interview them first. Find out how long they have been working with Reiki, and how many classes they have taught. Ask how they use Reiki in their life. Ask them to provide details of what their training programs consist of and what their fees are. Ask if the symbols you will learn are from the traditional Usui system.

When choosing a qualified Karuna Reiki® Master, it is a good idea to make sure that they are "Registered" with the International Center for Reiki Training. This is to insure that they will be complying with the teaching standards and the code of ethics. This also insures that they are to provide you with authorized training materials and that the attunements you receive will be from within the Karuna Reiki® tradition.

You can verify a teacher's registration by asking to see their certificate, which should have an official seal from the ICRT and a registration number. You can also verify their registration by emailing center@reiki.org and listing in the subject line "Karuna Reiki® registration verification".

After considering all these things, the most important method of determining whether a teacher is right for you is to follow your heart. If you feel empowered and supported by the way the teacher communicates with you, and if they have a loving, open, cooperative attitude regarding you and others in the Reiki community; those are good indications that you have found a teacher who is qualified to help you move forward on this sacred path.

If there isn't anyone in your local area that is qualified, or that you feel comfortable studying with, you may want to consider traveling to the right teacher. Embracing Reiki and Karuna Reiki® may be one of the most important steps in your life. It is a sacred experience that, when honored, and treated with reverence and commitment can enhance your relationship with Reiki for years to come.

Teach
Only Love

Karuna Reiki® Registration Program

Although Karuna Reiki® is a universal healing energy, the ICRT strives to maintain the integrity of the energy and the teachings by registering the name Karuna Reiki® as a trademark. This was done to protect recipients of the energy, as well as students seeking training.

Through the action of registering the trademark for Karuna Reiki®, the ICRT has established minimum teaching standards and a code ethics for practitioners and teachers to follow. ICRT maintains a Karuna Reiki® registration program that makes it simple to check the credentials of a person who practices or teaches Karuna Reiki®. If you would like to verify someone's registration status or register yourself, you can do so by contacting the International Center for Reiki Training (see the resource list in the back of this book).

Code of Ethics for Karuna Reiki Practitioners and Teachers

1. Agree with and work to fully express the Usui Ideals, the ICRT Philosophy and the ICRT Purpose.

2. Respect and value all Reiki practitioners and masters regardless of lineage or organizational affiliation. To refrain from making negative statements about other Reiki practitioners or masters.

3. Actively work to create harmony and friendly cooperation between all Reiki practitioners and masters regardless of lineage or organizational affiliation.

4. Encourage all students to use their own inner guidance in deciding who to receive Reiki treatments from or who to study Reiki with including the possibility of studying with more than one teacher.

5. Openly encourage all your clients and students to do the best job possible with the Reiki program they are guided to use.

6. Always work to empower your clients and students to heal themselves and to encourage and assist them in the their personal growth as well as in the development of their Reiki practice.

7. Always treat your students and clients with the greatest respect. Never engage in any illegal or immoral activity with your clients or students. Never touch their genital area or breasts, never ask them to disrobe, or never make sexual comments or references.

8. Abstain from the use of drugs or alcohol during all professional activities.

9. Practice Truth in Advertising. To be willing to openly discuss the subjects covered in your Reiki classes, the fee that is charged, and the amount of time spent in class with any prospective students. Ads should state what the student will be able to do upon completion of the class.

10. Never use another person's copyrighted material in your classes without permission and giving credit.

11. Be open to the continuing process of enhancing your professional qualifications, training, experience and skills.

12. Be actively working on your own healing so as to embody and fully express the essence of Reiki in everything you do.

13. Educate the client regarding the value of Reiki and explain that it does not guarantee a cure, and is not a substitute for medical or psychological treatment

14. Acknowledge that Reiki works in conjunction with other forms of medical or psychological care. If a client has a medical or psychological condition, suggest, in addition to giving them Reiki treatments, they see a health care practitioner if they are not already seeing one.

15. Never diagnose medical or psychological conditions or prescribe medications. Never suggest that a client change or end dosages of substances prescribed by other licensed health care providers or suggest the client change prescribed treatment or interfere with the treatment of a licensed health care provider.

Minimum Teaching Requirements for Karuna Reiki* Training

The ICRT requires all Registered Karuna Reiki Masters to teach according to Center guidelines. Below is a summary of the minimum teaching requirements.

<u>Classes must include the following subjects:</u>

- The history of Karuna Reiki
- Describe how to draw each symbol and have each student memorize them
- Describe how to activate the symbols
- Describe the uses for each symbol
- Give the Center attunement for each level taught
- Provide practice time in the use of each symbol
- If it is a master class, demonstrate and allow practice time for each attunement.
- Demonstrate and practice chanting and toning
- Conduct a written test on the symbols
- Provide the students with class review forms
- Issue certificates that are supplied by the ICRT, and explain the registration program.
- The official class manual published by the ICRT and Vision Publications must be provided for each student.

Minimum class time requirements

Karuna I Practitioner - 5-7 hours

Karuna II Practitioner - 5 - 7 hours

Karuna I Master - 5-7 hours

Karuna II Master - 5-7 hours

Karuna I & II Master 14-21 hours and a minimum of 2 days
(3 days recommended when there are more than 3 students)

Awakening to the Age of Peace

*"You may say I'm a dreamer,
but I'm not the only one
I hope someday you'll join us
and the world will live as one"
~John Lennon~*

Over the years I have come to know that peace isn't something that we need to search for, it isn't even something we need to "create" it is something that we all *are* inside.

Being peaceful is a choice that we can make. I find that it is easiest for me to be peaceful when I am living my life in a way that my needs are met, and that also makes a positive contribution to others.

There was a time that I thought I needed to make a positive contribution to others *before* I could consider my personal needs. I now understand that way of thinking contributes to the illusion of separation, which stands in the way of peace. Karuna Reiki' has helped me embrace Universal Love and Universal compassion. The more I learn to love and accept myself just as I am, the more natural being peaceful becomes. Healing is the result of opening to our innate ability to be peaceful. Karuna Reiki is a tool that helps us find that place of peace inside.

We are here on this planet to learn that it is actually very simple to *Be Love* and to *Be Peace*. We are here to awaken to the knowing that humanity has the power to live in peace, this very moment. Be Peace Now!

Om Shanti Gaia

Resources for Karuna Reiki®
Practitioners and Teachers

The International Center for Reiki Training
21421 Hilltop #28
Southfield, MI 48034
800-332-8112 or 248-948-8112
email: center@reiki.org   website: www.reiki.org

Laurelle Shanti Gaia
The Infinite Light Healing Studies Center, Inc.
P.O. Box 130
Hartsel, CO 80449
719-836-9385
email: Laurelle@ReikiClasses.com website: www.ReikiClasses.com

Michael Arthur Baird
Reiki Drumming™
P.O. Box 130
Hartsel, CO 80449
719-836-9385
email: Michael@ReikiClasses.com website: www.ReikiClasses.com

IARP-International Association of Reiki Professionals
P.O. Box 481
Winchester, MA 08190
781-729-3530
www.iarp.org

Eri Takase, Japanese Kanji Artist

www.takase.com

CD Journeys with Laurelle Shanti Gaia

Infinite Spectrum Chakra Journey
with Laurelle

Journey into the healing power of your soul using color, light and sound. Laurelle Gaia gently guides this healing journey on CD, that contains a 45 minute color energy session which can be used for relaxation, self empowerment and also used with clients.

Listen to this beautiful healing experience time and time again, and it can help you in new ways everytime you participate in it.

Includes CD, booklet and affirmation cards.
ISBN 0-9678721-1-1 $29.55

Sacred Circles . . . Journey into the angelic realms and inner planes
with Laurelle

Recorded LIVE at the Annual International Reiki Retreat.

Introducing The Sacred Circle and the Ascension Ring. Manifestation tools for aligning with the Divine and awakening to peace.

Learn to soul link with other lightworkers, Reiki guides and angels. Includes CD, booklet and affirmation cards. UPC 634479260421 $29.95

We are currently developing Reiki Review CDs, Reiki meditations and many more self development programs. Watch our online store for new releases www.ReikiClasses.com To order call us toll free 1-800-359-3424 or send an email to info@ReikiClasses.com.

Sacred Reiki
Retreats & Classes

An invitation from Laurelle & Michael

We would like to invite you to join us for Reiki, or Karuna Reiki classes, seminars or retreats. Our center is located in the remote mountains of Colorado where we hold many of our programs. We also arrange special classes at sacred sites, beaches, and energy vortexes around the world.

Our classes are internationally known for quality, integrity and respect for the sacred nature of Reiki.

It is always our goal to present programs that empower students, where we can share and exchange information openly and offer:

- Our 25 years of experience with subtle energies and spirituality including 14 years of daily Reiki practice
- Affilitation with the International Center for Reiki Trainig
- CEs and CEUs for nurses (AHNA) and Massage Therapists (NCBTMB)
- Ongoing support
- Original Japanese Reiki Techniques
- Personal research from Japan, Mt. Kurama and Usui Sensei's memorial
- Guidance to practice Reiki without rules, boundaries or fear
- Promotion of harmony in the Reiki community

Our retreats often include additional training and practice days, as well as special activities, like Reiki drumming instruction, and workshops where students make their own healing drum.

We schedule retreats in Sedona, mountain and tropical settings, as well as cruises, sacred sites, and other spiritual environments. Class sponsors are welcome. For a current schedule, or additional information, please visit our website or give us a call.

www.ReikiClasses.com email info@ReikiClasses.com
Infinite Light - P.O. Box 130 - Hartsel, CO 80449
719-836-9385 or 800-359-3424

Infinite Light Soul Profile Readings & Clearings

Soul profile readings can assist you in understanding your life purpose. Soul clearings can help eliminate confusion, and create a stronger sense of focus on the path of our soul's progression.

This can help when we feel "stuck", are in the midst of a life transition, or simply seeking more clarity and a sense of inner peace. These issues and more can be identified, and necessary clearings are recommended. Tap into the wisdom of your soul through your personal blueprint in the Akashic records.

Learn more about yourself:

- Which Soul Group are you from and what is their group mission?
- Which Archangel Realm did you incarnate through
- What is your soul type
- What is the condition of your soul memory system?
- Are you fully aligned with the Divine Temples?
- Are your spiritual guides working with you effectively?

These issues and more can be identified, and clearings are recommended. The clearings are performed only with the client's conscious and soul permission. All work is done using absentee, or distant healing energies. Reports are delivered via email or US Mail

Comments about this work . . .

"Laurelle, the soul reading you did for me was profound. I was in the midst of a major life change and the reading clarified some of the surrounding confusion. The 21 day clearing released old energy patterns and was very helpful. I recommend this work to anyone seeking a deeper understanding of their soul purpose. Laurelle, you are an integritious channel, thank you." Jan, RN, KRM

A comprehensive Reading/Clearing by Laurelle Gaia $225 (3 hrs) Includes detailed written report. Follow-up telephone consultations can be arranged for $40 for 1/2 hr. To schedule an appointment with Laurelle for a Soul Profile Reading and Clearing, call 719-836-9385 or email IAMInfiniteLight@aol.com

The Reiki Resource Center

www.ReikiBooksCDs.com

1-800-359-3424

OUR MISSION is to provide services, tools, products and resources that support the personal spiritual empowerment of Reiki practitioners, teachers and clients.

- ◆ Books on Reiki and spiritual topics
- ◆ Reiki and meditation CDs
- ◆ Massage Tables
- ◆ Reiki Tables
- ◆ Drums
- ◆ Reiki certificate service for Reiki Masters

and introducing the . . .

The Rejuvenation Table ... relax, release stress

Rejuvenate your clients & yourself!

Our "Rejuvenation Table" is crafted of high quality, durable, powder-coated steel. It is perfect for salons, spas and massage therapists to incorporate and provide a broader range of services to their client. Professional model $8,800 with payment terms available.

A rejuvenation session involves resting atop a thickly padded mattress and shifting into Aposition of perfect balance. A lightly scented herbal pillow is placed over your eyes to filter out bright light. Soft healing music surrounds you. The rejuvenation technician activates the table's smooth rotation, which is designed to take you deeper, and deeper into a state of complete relaxation. Our client's LOVE it . . .

"Each rejuvenation session is unique. Sometimes I feel as if I am floating in a sea of light . . . or . . . I feel as if I am totally weightless and being carried by a cloud. Regardless of the sensation, at the end of each session I always feel terrific!"

CPSIA information can be obtained at www.ICGtesting.com
Printed in the USA
BVOW061539160113

310673BV00002B/4/A